Succulents

Propagation

Attila Kapitany and Rudolf Schulz

ISBN 0 958516766

Schulz Publishing
Box 40, Teesdale, VIC 3328, Australia
tarrex@ozemail.com.au
gecko@connexus.net.au

Acknowledgements

We thank:
Cristina and Victor Aprozeanu, Austratec Pty Ltd, Anne Bartels, Bert and Mia Coppus,
Esme Dudley, Gary Dunn, Brian Gerrard, Kathleen Henderson,
Michele Kapitany, Marcel Maslin, Dane Sutton, Jan Welford and Warren Woolley

Printed in China by Everbest Printing Co Ltd

Preface

One of the most fascinating and enjoyable aspects of growing plants is producing new ones. We both independently started out as plant collectors, accumulating plants from around the world to admire and grow. As we had built up large, mostly potted collections, we learnt how to propagate our plants. In some cases, it was to rejuvenate them: in others, it was because they had outgrown their pots. Sometimes it was necessary to propagate just to save a little piece from a dying plant. Later, we became nurserymen, specialising in the propagation and growing of succulents of all types. Twenty-five years of experience in the nursery industry has taught us many lessons. In this book we share those lessons with you.

Attila Kapitany and Rudolf Schulz, Melbourne, Australia, 2004

The authors investigating cactus and succulent reproduction in a natural desert environment.

Contents

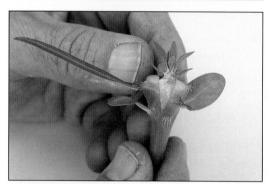

50   Seed raising

64   Propagation by genus

Propagation tips for forty-one specific groups of succulents (including cactus) are described in alphabetical order.

104   Appendix

How to propagate eighty popular succulents
How to propagate less common succulents
How to propagate less common cactus
Recommended reading

Introduction

Plant propagation is turning a single plant into two or more of the same. It can be replicating the parent exactly as in the case of a cutting or creating new plants altogether by raising them from seeds where the raised offspring may show slight differences from the parent plant.

Propagation is one of the most rewarding activities in the garden. The reasons gardeners propagate plants are numerous and varied. Here, we list some of the main reasons.

▸ Propagation is fun.
▸ Propagation creates a sense of personal achievement.
▸ Propagation is a creative extension of gardening.
▸ Many forms of propagation are very easy.
▸ Propagation is challenging, particularly the more advanced forms.
▸ Growing more of the same plant for use in mass plantings.
▸ Propagation is a way to recycle broken off pieces, as well as prunings.
▸ Propagation can save a dying plant.
▸ To help save a rare or endangered plant.
▸ New plants produced are great to share with friends.
▸ Propagation allows a more desirable plant to be replicated.
▸ Swapping spares with other growers.

⊻ Cuttings of succulents can often be obtained without cost. Within a few years a spectacular display like this can be achieved, the pots being the only expense. What price can you put on this sort of pleasure?

- It's economical! New plants are produced without having to buy any.
- It's a great fundraiser selling propagated plants.
- Propagation is excellent therapy in centres for rehabilitation and the disabled.

Some succulents are among the easiest of all plants to propagate, generally not involving any equipment, special place or training. Many can simply have stems broken off and immediately pushed into the ground. Then come the more challenging plants, which need some preparation, equipment and extra care. These are the most rewarding. Most of the more attractive, interesting and less common succulents seem to fall into this challenging category.

Success with propagation depends on a range of factors. The type of plant you want to reproduce will determine which method of propagation to use. Timing as to the right season to propagate may be the only difference between cuttings that grow roots in several weeks, or cuttings that just sit for months and eventually die.

Newly propagated plants may take weeks to months to develop enough roots to be self-sufficient. Hardening them off, which prepares them for the outside world or sunny exposed garden, may take a week or so. While no elaborate equipment is required, a shade house, greenhouse or glasshouse makes an

⩡ While some succulents are easy to propagate almost anywhere and at any time, lithops and many other more attractive succulents can only be grown from seeds which can be challenging.

excellent propagation environment; however, even an indoor windowsill or a simple plastic bag over a pot are excellent ways of giving plants extra care until they are ready for the outside world.

Where possible, propagation material should preferably come from healthy, fresh or new growth. Such cuttings will root more quickly and establish more successfully than propagation from diseased, weak or old tissue. Choose a good plant of a variety to propagate that shows the very best features that you would like to have more of. Direct cuttings from a parent with desirable traits will then guarantee an exact replica of the parent plant. Vegetative propagation (any propagation apart from seed raising) is also easier from juvenile plants than mature ones, because as a plant advances towards maturity its ability to reproduce vegetatively slowly declines.

Some succulents age quickly and weaken to an unhealthy state within just a few years. These plants generally benefit from a regular restart through propagation. While there are those that can naturally revitalise themselves and/or propagate themselves without any help, there are just as many plants that need 'encouragement' or even forced propagation.

Hybrids are only produced through cross-pollination between different species. The offspring are then selected for specimens which show improved qualities such as having bigger or brighter flowers. From these plants it is possible to reproduce the exact hybrid by vegetative propagation, that is, by simply taking cuttings. There are many hybrids and cultivars of echeverias and aeoniums which are superior in appearance to their wild relatives. These are only propagated from cuttings, as

trying to raise them from seeds usually results in very inferior plants.

There are usually a number of ways to propagate the same plant. In this book we have tried to identify the best methods for each type of succulent, however, in some cases plants may be propagated by other methods in your climate and with your particular conditions. Trying other methods is part of the challenge and fun of propagating.

One of the easiest ways to introduce children to the pleasures of gardening is to show them how to propagate succulents. They especially enjoy the tactile nature of the plants.

A cutting of *Crassula ovata* can grow into a great gift within one year. It is reputed to bring good luck, hence its nickname of 'lucky plant'. No luck is required to propagate this succulent.

A collector of rare haworthias carefully hand pollinates the flowers of a favourite species from which he wishes to obtain seeds.
Insert: Haworthia flowers average only 10 mm in diameter and require delicate handling in pollination.

Basic Propagation

Taking a cutting from a common 'hen and chickens' is something that most people feel comfortable doing without much effort, but there are other easy techniques which allow for many more succulent types to be propagated. All of these basic and easy propagation techniques can be carried out in an average garden without special equipment or facilities.

❤ Clean tools and equipment are most important. On the left are two unsatisfactory, rusty and unclean cutting implements which can easily transfer disease and viruses from cut to cut. Most home gardeners seem to get by with only clean kitchen utensils.

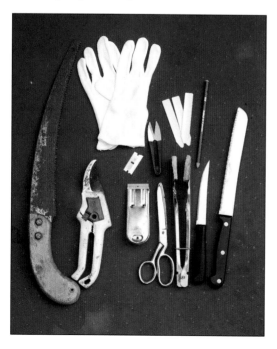

The propagation environment

For the home gardener or any newcomer to succulent propagation, all that is required is the kitchen sink, some kitchen utensils and a windowsill on which to grow all your new plants. From the occasional experiments growing on the windowsill, beginners usually progress to porches, verandahs or planting directly into the garden. As this is an infectious hobby, most who venture down this path soon end up with a specific area for propagation, whether indoors or out. While many may consider a greenhouse ideal for propagation, it is not essential.

There is no real measure as to what is ideal and what tools and equipment are required because it depends on two main factors – what type of succulent you wish to propagate and secondly what lengths and costs you are prepared to go to in order to achieve your objectives.

For propagation of succulents, we recommend:
▶ A comfortable and easy to use work area such as a bench at which to stand or sit.
▶ Clean or sterilised tools, pots, work area and potting mix.
▶ Healthy plants or seeds from which to propagate.
▶ A location that is protected from extreme climatic conditions.

⬆ The environment need not always be fancy or large. Here, some seedlings are growing well in a recycled food container kept on a well lit window sill.

⬆ A mini hot house for raising cuttings or seed. An old foam box can provide good insulation. A glass sheet over the top will help further by keeping in heat and humidity. If kept totally covered, avoid direct summer sun as cuttings and seedlings can cook.

⬇ The more time, effort and resources you have the better, especially for the less common succulents. Artificial light, heat pads and a clean environment are used here. The plastic bags are an easy way to control and maintain humidity and keep out pests.

Offsets

Offsets (a type of cutting) are small plantlets or branches which develop alongside the main body. They are usually smaller replicas of the main plant and are able to grow roots while still attached. Taking an offset is also commonly referred to as taking a cutting, even though no direct cut with an implement may be needed. Some types, such as the very common *Echeveria glauca* var. *pumila*, regularly produce offsets in such quantities that a single plant can produce several hundred new plants within two years. Others, such as the rare and slow growing *Echeveria laui*, may produce one offset every five years. There are techniques (see page 42) for propagating such plants by forcing offsets. Sometimes offsets, particularly those produced near soil level, will grow roots while still on the parent plant, making multiplication a simple matter of gently pulling or cutting the offset from the stem and shifting it to a new location or into a pot. In most instances, taking offsets is best done during spring and summer. Dense short stemmed rosette clumps usually need to be lifted from the garden or unpotted as this work is best done when unpotted or dug up. Often dead and old leaves need to be removed before the offsets can be detached. In some instances, as with many miniature aloes, offsets detach with only a slight nudge. You will need to experiment to find out how firmly these are attached to the parent plant and cut if necessary.

Freshly cut offsets without roots are best allowed to callous (dry out in air) before being placed in new potting mix or planted out directly into the garden.

⊼ One of the most common and easiest to propagate rosette succulents is *Echeveria glauca* var. *pumila*. Offsets are numerous and can be carefully pulled from the parent plant. Some may have roots already.

⊻ Most of these sempervivum offsets already have roots and need only to be cut or torn away from the parent plant. No drying or callous is required as the offsets can be planted and watered in immediately.

Bulbils and plantlets from flower stalks

Some succulents produce small plants called bulbils on their flower stalks irrespective of whether the flowers develop fruit and seeds. Bulbils are bulb-like in their stem shape. They can be produced in their hundreds and once they reach a substantial size, they are shed by the parent plant. Each bulbil has the beginnings of a root system and is capable of growing into a normal shaped plant. Furcraeas and some agaves are the best known succulents for producing bulbils.

Other succulents such as haworthias and gasterias produce occasional plantlets on their flower stalks, usually at the junction of the first flower. Often a small leaflet forms, later followed by a small plantlet which can take months to fully develop. Under natural conditions, such plantlets will continue to grow until their weight unbalances the flower stalk which then bends until the plantlet reaches the ground where it roots and grows independently. Bulbils and other plantlets can be removed and planted when large enough to handle easily or as flower stalks wither. No callous time is needed. For more advanced forms of propagation from flower stalks see page 37.

Some kalanchoes (formerly in the genus Bryophyllum) also grow plantlets but along the leaf margins as they mature and begin flowering. These can be very weedy and are a pest in many areas. We do not encourage their propagation.

⤴ Bulbils are small bulb-like plantlets which grow from the flower stalk on some agaves and furcraeas. As bulbils mature, they fall to the ground and form roots.

⤵ *Haworthia attenuata* occasionally grows a plantlet midway along a flower stalk. This one is an ideal size to pick off and plant separately.

Divisions

Multiplication of succulents by division is the separating of a plant clump into two or more pieces which have some roots attached. Dense clump forming succulents benefit from being periodically divided or cut apart as the original plant will often go into decline after some years. Often plants multiplied by division have no obvious parent plant. Instead, they consist of near uniform sized individual stems or bodies. In many instances, division is similar to taking offsets or stem cuttings, but true division involves dividing mature stems which already have developed root systems.

Sansevierias are a good example of where division is often used. With age, many sansevierias form dense clumps consisting of many individual, closely packed stems. While it is possible to take small individual cuttings of single stems from the edges of the clump, it is easier to completely lift and split the whole clump and then plant up the smaller clumps or individual stems. Often each stem will have its own roots and can be directly potted up or planted out. Division is best carried out in spring and summer. After repotting, do not water for a few days.

Plants which are often reproduced by division are sun hardy bromeliads, shrubby aloes, gasterias, sansevierias, some yuccas, haworthias, crassulas and stapeliads.

⬆ This *Haemanthus albiflos* is in need of repotting. Insert: Ripe fruit of *H. albiflos*. Flowers are self-fertile. A single seed is enclosed in each fleshy fruit. Ripe seeds need to be planted immediately.

⬇ Bulbs can be divided at any time of the year. Those with roots can be potted up immediately.

⬆ Many sansevierias form clumps which fill the pot to bursting. This specimen has been neglected for many years. Its pale, yellowish-green leaves indicate a lack of nutrients and the stems hanging over the pot rim show that this plant is in need of repotting.

⬆ The rootball can be sawn into convenient segments. While this appears radical, the use of a saw to divide the roots and stems is by far the quickest and easiest method. Some leaves, stems and roots will be damaged but almost all will eventually recover.

⬇ Division into varying sizes is possible. The size to cut should be determined by what size pots are available. The clump on the left can be divided further.

⬇ After one year, three of the segments shown in the picture on the left have grown into large plants which could be divided again. Note how the plants now have a dark green colour which reflects the fresh potting mix and nutrient content.

Runners and rhizomes

Several types of succulents produce offsets at the end of stems which can be above ground (runners) or remain below ground (rhizomes). Several kalanchoes produce plantlets on long, thin runners. Many common succulents such as *Senecio mandraliscae*, *S. serpens* and *Agave americana* are often propagated from rhizomes. Sometimes these types of offsets can develop over 1 metre away from the parent plant, leading some gardeners to assume that they are seedlings or just plants which have somehow established themselves. Careful digging on the parent plant side of such offsets will show that they are connected by a stout underground rhizome. In the garden, offsets can be cut from the parent plant at any time. The larger the offset, the larger the root system they will have on their own and the faster they will re-establish. Small offsets on rhizomes may not have any roots and in this case they need to be treated as cuttings before planting up.

Some species which produce rhizomes can be a problem (such as some agaves) as they can quickly infest the garden with numerous offspring which in turn will produce additional rhizomes until an impenetrable thicket is formed. For best appearance, keep such plants solitary by annually removing the rhizomes.

Some potted agaves will also produce rhizomes which can be a nuisance as they often emerge from the drainage holes at the bottom of the pot. This makes repotting difficult and it will often be necessary to destroy some of the new plants to loosen the main plant from its pot. When repotting, undeveloped rhizomes can sometimes be found growing from the parent plant. These can be detached, and if they have roots of their own, they can be planted with just

their white tips exposed to light. If done correctly, they will quickly turn green and form small plants.

Some sansevierias produce runners coming out from the parent plant to a distance of 300 mm or more. Allow such runners to form small plants before detachment.

⊼ *Sansevieria suffruticosa* is one of the species in this genus which produces above ground runners. Wait until these have at least five leaves and then cut off cleanly. Often roots will begin to develop while still on the parent plant.

⊻ Once large enough, these new plants growing on rhizomes can be dug up and cut away from the parent plant.

▲ The same *Agave americana variegata* (pictured left) has been carefully unpotted, revealing how the small plants are attached to the parent plant from rhizomes (underground stems).

▲ A variegated *Agave americana* in need of some work. The pot is weed infested and several rhizomes are coming out from the drainage holes and developing into new plants.

▼ The above plants ten months later. Two of the small plants were cut from the rhizomes, potted up and have now developed into plants which would make ideal gifts.

Plant selection

Agaves with profuse rhizome production quickly multipy, and as a result, will become a problem in gardens, developing into unmanageable spiny thickets. The plants producing the least rhizomes make the best plants for the garden. The over-production of fast reproducing succulents results in the least desirable clones (plant selections) becoming the most common. If you want a solitary growing succulent, it is likely to be a seedling rather than a plant produced from a rhizome. Succulents from rhizomes are common and cheaper than seed grown plants; however, plants raised from seeds are a much better investment in the long term.

Cuttings

Stem cuttings are the most common form of cutting. Most gardeners are familiar with taking stem cuttings from easy to 'strike' (root) plants such as pelargoniums. Taking a stem cutting usually refers to the removal (by snapping, snipping, cutting or sawing) of a side stem or branch. This method leaves the parent plant still more or less complete in general appearance. A variation on this theme is taking a cutting from a plant which has a solitary growth habit (see pages 23-25). When such plants have an elongated stem, it is possible to cut out the fresh growth tip only, which is at the very top of the plant. This method is primarily used to force the main stem to grow multiple new growths which elongate and develop into new stems. These in turn can be cut off for standard stem cuttings.

Extending the tip cutting theme further results in deheading (see pages 23-25). This is where most but not all of the growing head of tall leafy succulents such as echeverias are cut off from their otherwise bare old, woody stem. By leaving a few leaves on the remaining stem, the plant is encouraged to produce new shoots which develop into new rosettes. The cut off head can be treated as a general cutting. This method is only recommended for healthy and vigorously growing plants.

Traditionally, cuttings from succulents are cut and allowed to callous for a few days or weeks before being potted up or planted out into the garden. Most common succulent cuttings taken in spring root down very easily. As a general rule, the cheaper and more freely available a plant is, the easier it is to propagate by cuttings. The best time to take most cuttings is in spring and summer, but aeoniums, being winter growers, root better

⤒ Roots forming in air from an echeveria cutting which was taken five weeks earlier. Fresh cuttings should preferably be kept upright to callous and form roots in a location that is well lit but where no direct sun reaches the cut surface.

⤓ Freshly cut stem cuttings of *Aeonium 'Zwartkop'* and *Senecio mandraliscae* were placed in a glass of water during winter. Within weeks fresh roots were growing from each stem. This goes completely against the commonly held belief that all succulent cuttings need to be calloused before being planted. Any fresh cutting that roots in water will just as easily form roots in damp potting mix.
Insert: Roots from *Senecio mandraliscae*.

in autumn and winter, as do other winter growing (and therefore summer dormant) types.

Several generalisations can be made as to the 'do's' and 'don'ts' of growing from stem cuttings. It is best to take cuttings from new or last year's growth as opposed to old, thick or woody stems. Stem cuttings from younger and actively growing parts of plants always root faster and more successfully than those taken from older, weaker plants. Sometimes a favorite shrubby succulent, such as *Aeonium 'Zwartkop'*, rots near the soil line. It is often simpler to take stem cuttings than to try and root the main stem which is old and woody and not likely to produce new roots easily. It is best to try and cut at least two nodes (stem joints) with every stem cutting. Cut just below a leaf joint. Cuttings are best taken during the growing season when plants are in active growth.

Timing is important. Late spring through to early autumn is the best time for taking cuttings as these months are drier and warmer, offering the most reliable conditions for succulent propagation. Light levels are also important. Placing fresh cuttings in the full glare of the summer sun will almost always result in failure, especially for small cuttings. Cuttings need to grow new roots, requiring the use of their stored water. The less water lost through leaves and stems, the easier it will be for the cutting to re-establish. Many cuttings will produce roots without being planted and this method is recommended for some types as it reduces the risk of stem rot caused by overwatering of planted cuttings. Newly established cuttings should not be fertilised for several weeks after planting, so avoid the temptation to 'push' them along prematurely as this can damage young roots.

⬆ Old plants with leggy stems such as this *Aeonium 'Tricolor'* cannot be rejuvenated. It is best to restart the plant by take new cuttings of the best rosettes (see below).

⬆ Take cuttings with short stems as these establish faster than old, lower stems.
⬇ Cuttings form vigorous roots within three weeks.

Succulents often propagated by cuttings

plant name	season	cutting length	time to callous	time before handling	notes (see right)
Aeonium arboreum	autumn + winter	60 mm	none required	1-2 months	1
Aeonium 'Tricolor'	autumn + winter	40 mm	none required	1-2 months	1
Aeonium 'Zwartkop'	autumn + winter	50 mm	none required	1-2 months	1
Aeonium smithii	autumn + winter	40 mm	none required	1-2 months	1
Aloe arborescens	spring	150 mm	2-3 weeks	2 months	
Aloe juvenna	spring	60 mm	2-3 weeks	3 months	2
Aloe mitriformis	late spring	150 mm	1-2 months	6 months	2
Aloe plicatilis	late spring	250 mm	2-3 months	12 months	
Aloe x spinosissima	spring	150 mm	2-3 weeks	2 months	2
Aptenia cordifolia	spring + autumn	120 mm	2-3 days	1 month	5
Adenium obesum	summer	100 mm	none required	3 months	3
cactus	(see page 28 for details)				
Carpobrotus edulis	spring + autumn	120 mm	1-2 weeks	1 month	4, 5
Ceropegia sandersonii	spring + autumn	80 mm	none required	3 months	3
Ceropegia woodii	spring + autumn	80 mm	none required	3 months	3
Cotyledon orbiculata	spring + autumn	100 mm	2-3 weeks	3 months	5
Cotyledon macrantha	spring + autumn	120 mm	2-3 weeks	3 months	5
Cotyledon tomentosa	spring + autumn	100 mm	2-3 weeks	3 months	5
Crassula anomala	spring	30 mm	1-2 weeks	1-2 months	6
Crassula arborescens	spring	70 mm	2-3 weeks	3 months	6
Crassula 'Baby's Necklace'	spring	60 mm	2-3 weeks	3 months	6
Crassula corymbulosa	spring	50 mm	1-2 weeks	1-2 months	6
Crassula falcata	spring	80 mm	2-3 weeks	3 months	6
Crassula 'Gollum'	spring	60 mm	2-3 weeks	3 months	6
Crassula multicava	spring + autumn	40 mm	3-5 days	1 month	6
Crassula ovata	spring	80 mm	2-3 weeks	3 months	6
Crassula teres	spring-summer	30 mm	3-4 weeks	3 months	6
Delosperma species	spring + autumn	100 mm	2-3 weeks	3 months	2
Dudleya species (clustering)	autumn	50mm	2 weeks	12 months	2, 4
Echeveria 'Doris Taylor'	spring + autumn	60 mm	2-3 weeks	3 months	6
Echeveria multicaulis	spring + autumn	60 mm	2-3 weeks	3 months	6
Echeveria nodulosa	spring + autumn	40 mm	2-3 weeks	3 months	6
Echeveria pulvinata	spring + autumn	60 mm	2-3 weeks	6 months	6
Echeveria pulvinata 'Frosty'	spring + autumn	50 mm	2-3 weeks	6 months	6
Epiphyllum hybrids	late spring	140 mm	3-4 weeks	3 months	3
Euphorbia caput-medusae	spring + autumn	80 mm	2-3 months	12 months	7
Euphorbia enopla	late spring	60 mm	2-3 months	12 months	8
Euphorbia eritrea	summer	120 mm	2-3 months	12 months	3, 8
Euphorbia flanaganii	spring + autumn	60 mm	2-3 months	12 months	7

continued page 22

♠ Diseased plants such as this euphorbia, should not be used for propagation. Even though the lower stem appears to be free of infection, it almost certainly contains the disease.

♠ Watch for fallen or soft rotting leaves around the base of cuttings. Regularly remove these to prevent rot from infecting nearby leaves or plants.

▶▶ This echeveria appears to be producing a side stem, but it is actually a developing flower stalk which will only elongate and attempt to produce flowers. The stalk can still be used for propagation using a more advanced technique (see page 37).

Table details, page 20

<u>Season</u> refers to the best time to initiate propagation.
<u>Cutting length</u>: ideal length of stem, excluding leaves.
<u>Time to callous</u> refers to the time it takes for a cut surface to heal and be ready for planting.
<u>Handling</u> refers to the time it takes for new cuttings to be established well enough to repot or plant out.
<u>Notes</u>:
  1: Plant immediately and water.
  2: Peel off the lower 2-3 leaves, then dry.
  3: Keep warm and humid after planting.
  4: Do not bury stems.
  5: Take cuttings from fresh green stems.
  6: Remove flowers during propagation.
  7: Side branches will root without forming typical plants.
  8: Beware of caustic euphorbia sap.
  9: Keep away from humidity.
  10: Preferably cut at stem joints.

Succulents often propagated by cuttings, continued

plant name	season	cutting length	time to callous	time before handling	notes (see right)
Euphorbia grandicornis	late spring	200 mm	2-3 months	12 months	8
Euphorbia mammillaris	spring-autumn	80 mm	3 weeks	3 months	8
Euphorbia milii	late spring	80 mm	3-4 weeks	3 months	3, 8
Euphorbia trigona	summer	120 mm	2-3 months	12 months	8
Faucaria species	spring + autumn	30 mm	3-4 weeks	6 months	4, 9
Glottiphyllum species	spring + autumn	60 mm	3 weeks	3 months	2, 4
Graptopetalum paraguayense	spring + autumn	40 mm	1-2 weeks	1-2 months	2, 6
Hoya australis	late spring	100 mm	none required	2 months	3
Hoya carnosa	late spring	100 mm	none required	2 months	3
Kalanchoe blossfeldiana	summer	50 mm	1-2 weeks	1-2 months	5, 6
Kalanchoe fedtschenkoi	summer	60 mm	1-2 weeks	2 months	5, 6
Kalanchoe marmorata	summer	60 mm	2-3 weeks	2 months	2, 5, 6
Kalanchoe pumila	summer	40 mm	1-2 weeks	1-2 months	6
Kalanchoe tomentosa	summer	60 mm	2-3 weeks	3 months	5
Lampranthus species	spring + autumn	100 mm	3-5 days	1 month	6
Orbea variegata	summer	segment	2 weeks	3 months	4, 10
Oscularia deltoides	spring + autumn	100 mm	1-2 weeks	1-2 months	6
Pachyphytum compactum	spring	40 mm	3-4 weeks	6 months	9
Pachyphytum oviferum	spring	40 mm	3-4 weeks	6 months	9
Portulacaria afra	spring + autumn	100 mm	2-3 weeks	3 months	5
Sedum burrito	spring + autumn	40 mm	2-3 weeks	3 months	2
Sedum dasyphyllum	autumn + winter	20 mm	none required	1 month	2
Sedum mexicanum	autumn + winter	30 mm	none required	1 month	2, 5
Sedum morganianum	spring + autumn	40 mm	2-3 weeks	3 months	2
Sedum nussbaumerianum	spring + autumn	40 mm	2-3 weeks	3 months	2
Sedum pachyphyllum	spring + autumn	40 mm	1-2 weeks	3 months	2
Sedum praeltum	spring + autumn	50 mm	1-2 weeks	2 months	
Sedum rubrotinctum	spring + autumn	40 mm	1-2 weeks	2 months	2
Sedum sieboldii	spring	20 mm	none required	1 month	5
Sedum spathulatum	spring + autumn	30 mm	1-2 weeks	1-2 months	4
Sedum spectabile	spring	40 mm	none required	1 month	5
Sedum 'Vera Jamieson'	spring	40 mm	none required	1 month	5
Senecio haworthii	summer	60 mm	3-4 weeks	6 months	2
Senecio mandraliscae	autumn + winter	120 mm	none required	1-2 months	2
Senecio petrae	spring	80 mm	2-3 weeks	1-2 months	
Senecio rowleyanus	spring + autumn	100 mm	none required	2 months	
Senecio serpens	autumn + winter	50 mm	none required	1-2 months	2
Stapelia gigantea	summer	segment	2 weeks	3 months	4, 10
Yucca aloifolia	summer	200 mm+	1-2 months	12 months	2
Yucca elephantipes	summer	200 mm+	1-2 months	12 months	

Cutting guide for solitary plants

With solitary plants, where the actual cut is made along a stem is crucial in determining the outcome. Here are some possibilities.

A. Cutting here is known as pinching out. The aim of this technique is to pinch or cut out the growing point in order to force side stems which are then recut as stem cuttings. The 'pinched out' cutting is always discarded. This method does the least amount of visual damage to the plant. Such plants often develop into spectacular multiheaded clumps.

B. Sometimes called deheading. If cut here, the cutting is large enough to root and establish as a plant. Taking a cutting here will force new shoots on the remaining stem. A few leaves left on the stem enable the old stem to recover and for multiple new stem growth to develop. This method produces the most new stems.

C. Called deheading. Cutting here will produce a complete head that roots easily. The remaining stem will wither slowly and may produce a few offsets.

D. Sometimes called deheading. Taking a cutting here will result in a sizeable stem attached. This common method is not recommended because it produces poor head cuttings that establish slowly. The lower stem will usually wither and die, producing one or two offsets at the most.

E. Taking a cutting here is not recommended. The upper portion will root poorly and grow slowly and the lower, old woody stem will die without producing offsets.

Table details, page 22

<u>Season</u> refers to the best time to initiate propagation.
<u>Cutting length</u>: ideal length of stem, excluding leaves.
<u>Time to callous</u> refers to the time it takes for a cut surface to heal and be ready for planting.
<u>Handling</u> refers to the time it takes for new cuttings to be established well enough to repot or plant out.
<u>Notes</u>:
  1: Plant immediately and water in.
  2: Peel off the lower 2-3 leaves, then dry.
  3: Keep warm and humid after planting.
  4: Plant no deeper than 10 mm.
  5: Take cuttings from fresh green stems.
  6: Remove flowers during propagation.
  7: Side branches will root without forming typical plants.
  8: Beware of caustic euphorbia sap.
  9: Keep away from humidity.
10: Preferably cut at stem joints.

Head cuttings

Deheading is a form of stem cutting. This method is often used with frilly echeveria hybrids which grow as solitary plants that after a few years become weaker as they rise on tall stalks. Their stems often lean or fall over, making the whole plant unsightly. Deheading is the primary way to rejuvenate and re-establish such plants. Deheading is best done in spring.

After deheading, the cut off rosette needs to be left to dry for at least a week in order to form a callous. It can then be planted into good potting mix or laid on the surface of the soil in the garden where it will form roots.

The lower stem can be used for propagation as it will form new plantlets, but only if cut correctly (see page 23).

◀ Deheading echeverias is best done with a sharp knife. Wash or sterilise the knife after cutting between plants to avoid spreading viruses.

▶▶ Before a callous forms, the exposed wound and undersides can be easily sunburnt. Keep them out of the sun and rain for at least a week. See page 35 for an alternative method of storage.

▶▶ Insert: A dry crusted callous has developed after ten days, indicating it is ready to plant.

◀ Head cuttings with root development after four weeks. These cuttings are now ready for planting.

Short stemmed head cuts

A number of aloes grow as single rosettes and remain more or less stemless throughout their lives. *Aloe polyphylla* is one of the most desirable single-stemmed species which requires this method to obtain offsets. Plants will not grow from leaves and usually do not produce offsets even at an advanced age. The simplest way to propagate such plants is to dehead them as shown in these photographs. If the rosette is cut too low down, the lower stem will quickly die as it may not have enough leaves to ensure its survival. If cut too high, the growing point may be damaged and the cutting will die. When correctly done, the top portion will root as a large cutting and the lower stem will produce numerous offsets which can be removed once they are 80-120 mm in diameter. Some offsets will already have small roots developing even before they are cut away. This technique is not well suited to hard or stiff leafed succulents such as most agaves because it will be extremely difficult to separate the head cleanly from the remaining body.

◥ A helper is needed to hold half of the leaves up and the rest down. A filleting knife is the ideal cutting tool. Alternatively, a long bladed bread knife will do the job. If correctly cut, the two portions come apart with an equal number of leaves. Remove any leaves that have been damaged by the cutting blade and loosely cover the cut area with shadecloth to avoid sunburn. Note that the inner tissue is a very pale green or white, indicating that it is susceptible to sunburn. Keep both wounds dry for about four weeks. The top cutting can then be placed onto damp potting mix to root.

▸▸ Three months later. The lower stem is developing an offset.

Cuttings from crested, monstrose and variegated plants

Succulents occasionally deviate from normal growth and develop mutations. These take on three main forms – a crest (cristate), a monstrose or a variegate. If desirable, such forms can be propagated vegetatively by stem cuttings.

⬇ Choose variegated cuttings carefully as stem cuttings with little or no green colour will usually die (as with the central rosette in this picture). Take stem cuttings which have balanced proportions of the green parts needed for photosynthesis. If you wish to maintain this variegated aeonium cultivar, the excessively green or yellow stems should be cut out and discarded.

Crests

A crested plant has an elongated growing point which causes the stem to widen and eventually distort. Crests are thought to be difficult to grow on their own roots and have traditionally been grafted. Most produce roots from stem cuttings and so are easily propagated this way.

Crested succulents, especially cactus, suffer when new growth fans out, often causing it to grow towards the ground or into the potting mix. This turning of the growing apex results in the plant being pushed out of the ground by its roots. Where the new growth touches the damp soil, rot or disease will easily set in. Because of this, crests are generally a little more demanding and are usually restarted from fresh cuttings every few years.

Monstrose

A monstrose plant exhibits unusual growth which may take many different forms. Monstrose plants propagate well from stem cuttings.

Variegates

A variegated plant lacks the green pigment in some leaf or stem section and usually has white or yellow stripes or streaks. Should a stem on a succulent develop which is all yellow or white, then it is almost certain that trying to reproduce it from cuttings will fail. The more yellow or white in proportion to the amount of green, the less chance the cuttings will have of surviving as plants. The best cuttings from variegated plants are from stems which have an almost equal balance between green and non-green portions. Variegated succulents are usually grown on their own roots, while cactus are often grafted.

⬆ *Sedum praeltum* ssp. *dendroideum* has a crested form which regularly reverts to the normal form (pictured in the centre). The two plant forms look very different but are genetically almost identical.

⬇ *Mammillaria bocasana 'Fred'* is a strange monstrose cactus (see insert). It grows well from cuttings taken during the warmer months of the year and allowed to callous for a few weeks before being planted in damp potting mix. If potted up too early, some of the cuttings may rot. If allowed to callous for too long, many of the cuttings dry out and fail to root. With propagation, timing is everything and comes with experience aided by good record keeping.

⬇ Plants purchased as crests may revert to their original form. In the picture below, the crest is in the centre and is being rapidly taken over by normal stems. Normal stems should be cut away each spring to prevent them from crowding out the slower developing cristate. Crested plants which revert like the one below are useful because they can supply two types of plants for cuttings, the crested form and a normal form.

Cactus often propagated by cuttings

genus	best method of propagation	difficulty	comments
Aporocactus	stem cuttings	easy	1, 7,
Cereus	stem cuttings	easy	1, 4, 6
Chamaecereus	offsets	easy	1, 7,
Cleistocactus	stem cuttings	easy	4, 6
Copiapoa	offsets	moderate	5, 7 Small growing species.
Coryphantha	offsets	moderate	5
Echinocereus	stem cuttings	moderate	Branching species only.
Echinopsis	offsets	easy	7
Epiphyllum	stem cuttings	easy	1, 2, 3, 7
Gymnocalycium	offsets	moderate	Smaller clumping species only.
Hylocereus	stem cuttings	easy	1, 2, 7
Lobivia	offsets	moderate	
Mammillaria	offsets	moderate	5
Myrtillocactus	stem cuttings	moderate	4, 6
Notocactus	offsets	easy	5
Opuntia	stem cuttings	easy	Small spines, handle carefully.
Pereskiopsis	stem cuttings	easy	2, 3, 7
Pilosocereus	stem cuttings	moderate	4, 6
Rebutia	offsets	easy	5
Rhipsalis	stem cuttings	easy	1, 2, 3, 7
Schlumbergera	stem cuttings	easy	1, 2, 3, 7
Sulcorebutia	offsets	easy	5
Trichocereus	stem cuttings	easy	4, 6 Branching species only.

Table details above

Best method of propagation is usually the easiest method. However, all the genera can also be propagated via seeds.

Difficulty refers to how easy or hard the more common species of the genus are to propagate.

Comments: see below.

1: Remove flowers during propagation.
2: Prefers humidity.
3: Light shade during propagation.
4: Saw required for woody stems.
5: From those species which clump.
6: Slow rooting (usually four or more months).
7: Short callous time (1-2 weeks only).

⍗ Stem cuttings of tall growing cactus lying on their sides to callous for four months. During this period they have flowered (note remains of dried flowers).

Cactus cuttings

Taking cuttings of cactus may involve cutting with a knife or a saw blade but the removal of offsets often does not require any cut to be made. Some types have easily detachable stem parts that just fall away with a gentle touch while others may need force or even an incision at the base where offsets join the parent plant. The easier that offsets or stem cuttings come away from the parent plant, the easier and quicker they are likely to establish as new plants on their own. The best time to take cactus cuttings is mid to late spring.

Generally a callous period is needed after taking cuttings of most cactus. The larger the cut surface area on any cactus cutting, the longer the callous time. In cooler climates, large stem cuttings of cactus are left to callous in an upright position for up to twelve months and then planted in the following spring, whether they have roots or not. Cereus forms and epiphyllums that are laid on their side for more than a few weeks will often bend out of shape.

In cooler climates many books recommend dusting open wounds with sulphur powder to help seal and prevent disease from entering. We have successfully taken thousands of cactus cuttings and have never used sulphur at all. In poor climatic conditions or in emergency situations to save a piece of a dying plant, use sulphur powder on the cut. Take the cutting indoors and dry it out near the vent of a heater for several weeks. Plant it out in the following spring.

Never bury cactus cuttings deeply into potting mix as this encourages stem rot. Rather, rest them on the potting mix and prop them up temporarily with stakes or small rocks until established. This is most helpful with taller and top heavy types of cactus. With shorter, globular types, gently push into potting mix until a shallow depression is made that is just deep enough to support them in an upright position. Cactus cuttings are mostly free of pest and disease problems if clean cuts are taken from clean healthy plants.

⍢ After six weeks of drying in a tray, these cuttings are just starting to show root development. An extended callous period of 4-6 weeks is the minimum for most large cactus stem cuttings.

Leaf Propagation

Many succulents can be grown from single leaves which fall off, are shaken off, are broken off or are cut away from a parent plant. These are often referred to as leaf cuttings (even though a cut is not always necessary). Leaf cuttings will develop into miniature versions of the original plant. Multiplication of succulents from leaves is best carried out in the warmer months. Winter growers like *Aeonium tabuliforme* are best done in autumn.

Smaller growing sedums, echeverias and related genera are most commonly propagated from leaf cuttings. Their leaves root rapidly and form plantlets (miniature versions of the original plant). Many species, including haworthias and gasterias, will root and produce plantlets only very slowly, or only when given just the right conditions. As a result, these types are far less common in cultivation than the easy-to- multiply types. In between these two extremes of easy and difficult are hundreds of types which gardeners and succulent collectors can multiply from leaves.

Leaves should be removed carefully from the lower stem. They need to retain as much of the leaf baseas possible, because this is where the growth tissue is. Lower leaves which show any signs of discolouring or withering will fail, so discard these first before removing some healthier leaves.

Detached leaves need a callousing period, ranging from a few days to several weeks. They should be kept in bright light but out of direct summer sunlight, especially on days of very high temperatures. Spread

⬆ Echeveria leaves showing new root and plantlet formation. Note the label with propagation details.

⬆ A selection of plantlets produced from leaves.

⬇ Some fleshy leafed succulents drop living leaves readily. Often these will establisheasily as new plants where they fall to the ground.

them out in a dry, shallow container. Once leaves show the first signs of growing roots, shoots (or both), they should be carefully planted or laid on to damp potting mix and then given a light watering or misting. When new plantlets appear they should be given more frequent watering and gradually given more light. A single leaf cutting can often produce multiple plantlets which can later be divided into single plants once they have grown to larger than thumbnail size. Under ideal conditions, a single mature Echeveria 'Black Prince' can produce over 500 small plantlets within a year from leaf cuttings.

Propagation from leaves of some rosette types and sedums is easy and obvious. The leaves of a wide variety of other succulents can also be used. Some of these require a longer period to form plantlets. Some species such as kalanchoes and sansevierias have leaves which can be cut into sections. Leaves can be stored without being stuck in potting mix until the first signs of roots are evident. They can then be potted up to develop plantlets.

▶▶ Leaves from different plants often display a wide range of growth behaviour. All these leaves were removed about six weeks before photographing. Whereas the upper leaves have mostly grown new roots, the lower leaves have grown new shoots ahead of any root development.

⬆ Leaves from many succulents have a natural banana-like bend and while left to callous may bend considerably more. Plant these 'bend side' up or on their sides to reduce this problem. Do not bury leaves for support; rather, lean them against the edge of the pot or tray, especially for larger, thick leafed forms which can rot easily if in too much contact with damp potting mix. Only the base of the leaf needs to be in contact with the potting mix.

Succulents often propagated from leaves

plant name	season	strike rate	time before handling	height+width after 1 year	notes (see right)
Aeonium tabuliforme	autumn	high	6 months	10 x 100 mm	
Adromischus cooperi	spring	moderate	12 months	40 x 30 mm	10
Cotyledon orbiculata	spring + autumn	low		no growth	6
Echeveria agavoides	summer	moderate	12 months	40 x 50 mm	
Echeveria 'Black Prince'	spring + autumn	high	6 months	50 x 90 mm	4
Echeveria 'Blue Curls'	summer	low	8 months	50 x 90 mm	3
Echeveria 'County Fair'	summer	low	8 months	80 x 100 mm	3
Echeveria globulosa	spring + autumn	high	3 months	30 x 50 mm	
Echeveria 'Golden Glow'	summer	moderate	6 months	70 x 100 mm	2
Echeveria laui	late spring	low	12 months	20 x 40 mm	5
Echeveria lilacina	late spring	moderate	8 months	30 x 60 mm	
Echeveria 'Mauna Loa'	summer	low	6 months	80 x 120 mm	3
Echeveria 'Paul Bunyan'	summer	low	8 months	50 x 100 mm	3
Echeveria setosa	summer	moderate	6 months	40 x 60 mm	
Echeveria shaviana	spring + autumn	high	6 months	30 x 60 mm	
Echeveria 'Violet Queen'	spring + autumn	moderate	6 months	40 x 50 mm	
Echeveria 'Zorro'	summer	low	8 months	80 x 100 mm	3
Gasteria excelsa	late spring	moderate	12 months	60 x 80 mm	
Graptopetalum bellum	spring	high	8 months	20 x 40 mm	5
Graptopetalum paraguayense	spring + autumn	high	6 months	60 x 80 mm	
Graptoveria 'Debbi'	spring + autumn	high	8 months	40 x 60 mm	
Graptoveria 'Douglas Huth'	spring + autumn	high	6 months	50 x 80 mm	
Haworthia retusa	spring + autumn	moderate	12 months	20 x 20 mm	
Haworthia tesselata	spring + autumn	moderate	12 months	20 x 20 mm	
Kalanchoe beharensis	summer	high	6 months	160 x 160 mm	7
Kalanchoe fedtschenkoi	summer	high	2 months	120 x 60 mm	
Kalanchoe tomentosa	summer	high	3 months	100 x 60 mm	
Kalanchoe rhombopilosa	summer	high	2 months	70 x 30 mm	
Pachyphytum compactum	spring+autumn	high	6 months	60 x 40 mm	
Pachyphytum oviferum	spring + autumn	moderate	6 months	50 x 50 mm	
Sansevieria trifasciata	summer	moderate	8 months	150 x 50 mm	7
Sedum dasyphyllum	spring + autumn	high	2 months	30 x 30 mm	9
Sedum mexicanum	spring + autumn	moderate	2 months	70 x 200 mm	9
Sedum morganianum	spring + autumn	high	3 months	200 x 20 mm	
Sedum nussbaumerianum	spring + autumn	moderate	3 months	100 x 40 mm	
Sedum rubrotinctum	spring + autumn	high	4 months	70 x 120 mm	
Sinocrassula yunnanensis	spring + autumn	high	3 months	30 x 40 mm	
Sempervivum (large types)	spring	moderate	8 months	50 x 140 mm	2
Senecio mandraliscae	autumn + winter	low		no growth	6

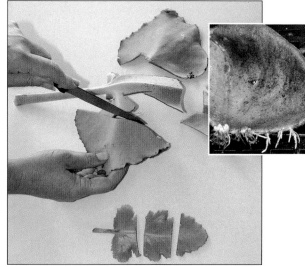

⬆ Leaves from variegated or pale clones such as this *Sedum rubrotinctum 'Aurora'* do not grow true to type. *'Aurora'* has pale, pinkish leaves. The fast growing green leafed plant among these stem cuttings has grown from a pale pink leaf that fell to the ground.

⬆ Many of the larger growing kalanchoes (and some crassulas) will produce plantlets from the midrib and from around the cut edges of their leaves. Here, a *Kalanchoe beharensis* leaf is being cut into sections, each of which will be placed on damp potting mix to root and produce plantlets.

⬇ *Kalanchoe beharensis* can grow leaves over 300 mm in length. Because of their size, they need special care. Plant each leaf in a pot as seen here, or cut into pieces (top picture) to make them more manageable.

Table details, page 32

Season refers to the preferred time to start propagation.

Strike rate refers to the average success rate.

Handling refers to the time it takes for new cuttings to be established well enough to repot or plant out.

Size at one year gives an approximation of how large the plant can grow with careful growing.

Notes:

 1: Leaves come away easily and grow where they fall.

 2: Leaves must be peeled away.

 3: Cut a little part of the stem with each leaf.

 4: Leaflets from flower stalks can be used as cuttings.

 5: Sensitive to overwatering, disease and pests.

 6: Leaves grow roots but seldom produce plantlets.

 7: Parts of leaves can grow new plantlets.

 8: Do not propagate in hot, dry weather.

 9: Immediately sprinkle leaves onto soil or potting mix.

10: Callous leaves for two weeks before planting.

Caring for cuttings and offsets

The period between taking a cutting and when it is established with a functioning root system is crucial. During this time the environment in which cuttings are kept and raised must be controlled. Keep cuttings out of the wind, away from direct sunlight and protect them from excessive temperature swings. The common species will be the least demanding, while the rarer, collectors' plants often require more precise control of the above points.

While most succulents are remarkably resistant to drying out, they still dehydrate faster when in dry air. Wind also causes cuttings to dry out, so keep cuttings in containers or areas which protect them from wind.

Sunlight is necessary for plant growth but excessive sunlight will increase drying out of cuttings as well as possibly burning leaves or stems. This is especially common with cuttings taken from areas of the plant which sunlight seldom reaches, such as stems from among foliage or from the shady side of plants. If such cuttings are exposed to intense sunlight they will easily burn. A suitable sunscreen is a piece of shade cloth draped over fresh cuttings, especially on very hot or sunny days.

Keeping the temperature within ideal limits is the most difficult thing for the home gardener to control. In commercial nurseries, all sorts of devices are available to control temperature, both cooling and heating. Keen readers may have noted that we seldom recommend summer as a time for propagation from leaves or stem cuttings. This is because summer temperatures in many locations are excessive and can inhibit or reduce the success of root formation and establishment. The best temperature for most propagation is 20-25°C by day and 15-20°C by night. While spring or autumn temperatures during the daytime often reach this, night temperatures are often too low. To compensate for this, use a foam container to insulate the cuttings or developing plants from the cool night air. Another simple solution is to bring cuttings into the house for the night, but do remember that they need much more light during the day than most indoor environments can provide. For keen propagators, we recommend a small electric heat pad (use only those sold specifically for propagating plants). These can be set to any desired temperature and will allow propagation even when the temperature is too low. But they do not solve the problem of excessively high temperatures. Luckily, almost all succulents are much more tolerant of high temperatures than low, so they will endure a few days of up to 35°C without any noticeable slowdown in growth.

Calloused cuttings can be planted into damp potting mix that is never allowed to completely dry out but is also not kept too wet or humid either. Roots soon follow once calloused cuttings are placed in damp potting mix. Once a functioning root system has grown, the cutting is an independent plant and can be potted up or planted out in the garden.

▲ A freshly cut tephrocactus cutting rests on a pot's edges. This keeps it in an upright position as well as keeping the base of the stem dry while callousing. Plant the cuttings when roots become visible. This technique can be used for a variety of succulents.

▼ Stem cuttings of *Graptopetalum superbum*. The lowest is freshly cut, the middle has been calloused for eight days. Note that the stem diameter is now smaller and the surface appears harder. The top cutting has been calloused for two weeks and is ready for planting. Insert: Closeup of rooting stem. Note that the roots grow from the leaf axis and not from the end of the stem.

Using sulphur and rooting hormones

Many books recommend the application of powdered sulphur on all plant cuttings or wounds. Other than in extremely cool or humid environments or when cuttings are taken during rainy weather, the use of powdered sulphur is unnecessary.

Many older books and articles on propagation advocate the use of rooting hormones, either in liquid or powder form, to speed up the formation of new roots on cuttings. We have found them unnecessary for succulents. These compounds may be of help in some cases, but be careful when using them as they contain poisonous chemicals.

Callous and root formation

After a cut is made, a drying time is required to seal the cut area. As the surface dries, it hardens to a crust which is called a callous. The formation of a callous on succulent cuttings is dependent on a number of factors. The lower the humidity and the warmer the temperature, the more rapidly a callous will form. It can take from several days to several weeks for this to happen. The intention is to have the cutting wound dry out to prevent disease or rot from entering the stem.

Plants with vigorous growth often form new roots quickly and do not need a callous time before planting. In many cases, it is not uncommon for roots to begin to develop from the base of cuttings even before the callous has formed. This is a very good sign of healthy recovery and an indication that the cuttings can be planted.

Advanced propagation

So far, we have looked at those easy and quick techniques which can be applied to plants without significantly damaging them. Unfortunately, many of the most desirable, expensive and rare plants cannot be quickly or easily propagated. In some cases, a more radical approach is required, which may ultimately destroy the parent plant but not before producing numerous new stems. Other techniques, such as grafting, are not as destructive but require a steady hand, sharp tools and some special after-care.

▲ These four haworthia seedlings have been selected because of their exceptional markings. To propagate them will require specialised techniques because they will not easily offset or produce removable leaves.

▲ Most propagation techniques only mimic what can occur in nature. This *Aeonium undulatum* normally grows as a single rosette on a tall bare stem. A heavy frost has killed the growth tip and all the leaves, causing the plant to produce numerous side stems.

▼ An animal has eaten this normally single stemmed echeveria to the ground. Note the regrowth. This is similar to forced propagation.

Advanced leaf propagation

Leaves that detach and grow new plants are called leaf cuttings (see page 30). An advanced form of leaf propagation requires a cut to be made, preferably with a scalpel or a razor blade. Some succulents, especially rosette succulents, have varieties which respond very poorly to normal leaf propagation. There are also those where detaching a leaf is not possible as they may be too brittle or fragile to handle. Experienced propagators have found that leaves can be cut away easily with a razor sharp blade. With each leaf a small sliver of stem from the parent plant is also cut. The purpose of this is to include the bud which lies at the base of a leaf. To do this effectively the plant being propagated should be unpotted and turned on its side or upside down. At least several older leaves are cut away before the younger and healthier leaves are reached. The closer the cut is to the apex, the more successful it will be. Leaf cuttings taken this way can then be treated as for all cuttings. Plants that propagate well by this method are the large frilly echeveria hybrids.

☟ A razor blade is used to cut *Echeveria subsessilis* leaves away with a small slice of stem attached.

☝ Flower stalk leaves. For difficult types we recommend that a small section of the stem should be carefully sliced off together with the leaf as this ensures that the growing point is attached and undamaged.

☟ An echeveria flower stalk has had all its flower buds removed. This forces liquids and nutrients that are normally used in flower development to well up in the stalk and leaflets. As long as all flowers are continually removed, a few plantlets may develop. Insert: Secondary flower buds. Remove these as they appear.

Plants from roots

Every collector with more than twenty different succulents is likely to have experienced trouble growing a special plant. It may even have died. It is worthwhile checking the potting mix afterwards to find out why the plant suffered in the first place. Occasionally there are roots or a buried stem still alive and healthy. As well, while repotting large healthy succulents, or while dividing clumps, roots may break or detach.

A number of succulents will grow plants from pieces of root. As a general rule, the thicker the root, the easier it will be to propagate. Using roots for propagation is a very slow process as roots will often take up to six months to show the first indications of a plant bud and at least one year to form a sizeable plant. Root cuttings are best taken in late spring. The larger and more complete or entire the roots are to begin with, the more likelihood of success.

Root propagation is easiest if the root still has a piece of stem attached. With a steady hand and using a scalpel, a tiny slice of stem cut away with a large root can be a wonderful way to experiment with all kinds of succulents.

Some plants which propagate well from roots are:
haworthias (all fat rooted species)
euphorbias (can be slow and difficult)
adenias
operculicaryas
cucurbits

⤊ *Euphorbia ornithopus* roots with new plantlets. The roots were cut from an old plant thirteen months earlier. Note the lighter root section which was above ground.

⤋ The swollen roots of *Haworthia* species can be forced to produce new plantlets from roots alone. Once unpotted, healthy, fat roots can be gently detached from the plant using a rocking and twisting motion. Detached roots should be planted as soon as possible in damp potting mix so that only the top 10 mm is exposed to light. Some roots will respond by growing several small new plantlets. Be patient! Sometimes this takes six to eight months.

⏶ Large plants of *Adenia fruticosa* often produce thick roots which can be used for propagation. The light coloured portion indicates the root section that was left above ground. Note how the new plants are coming up from lower down, not from the exposed root section. Once the new plants grow stronger and develop their own root system they can be carefully detached and potted separately. Insert: Adult plant.

⏷ *Operculicarya decaryi* root cuttings often grow new stems horizontally in contrast to seed grown plants which mostly grow upright stems.
Insert: Seed grown *O. decaryi*.

Record keeping

Propagation of succulents is a pleasurable gardening activity in itself and will provide hours of enjoyment as progress is noted and plants begin to grow. Gardeners who regularly propagate plants find record keeping helpful, especially if more successful propagation can be achieved next time. From seed to the development of a new plant is a long time and much of the reason and technique may be forgotten or lost, not to mention even the identity of the plant itself. It is worth keeping a record of the date of propagation, the type of plant (if it dies, at least you will know what that dead stick in the pot is!) and the number of propagations or seeds. The latter will help decide how successful the technique was. All of this information can be written on a label and it is also worthwhile to record the same information in a small notebook. This will help as a reference for when and how to propagate in years to come as well as providing information to friends who may also want to also learn the skills of plant multiplication.

Plant pot labels are normally plastic, which degrades and becomes brittle in a few years. The labels then disintegrate, especially if succulents are grown in high light areas. If plastic labels are not replaced valuable information will be lost. For best results, use aluminium labels which will last virtually forever. If these are not available, why not make your own from old venetian blind segments, which can be cut to size with scissors.

Pot plants can lose their labels for a variety of reasons. To ensure identification, why not place a plastic label at the bottom of each pot when repotting? Even if the main label is lost or unclear, the secondary label will always be there.

Surgical division

Single rosettes which seldom offset can be cut into segments and allowed to callous. After a few weeks, new stem shoots is often produced. Some very rare or slow growing types can only be propagated by being dismembered and completely cut into pieces.

Surgical division is best done in spring because the cut pieces are slow to callous and form plantlets. The aim is to have rooted pieces by autumn which will survive the dormant winter period better than just calloused pieces.

Some plants which can be propagated by surgical division are haworthias, aloes and echeverias.

This *Haworthia retusa* rosette will have about 70% of its body cut off.

The upper portion that was cut away is cut up from below, so as to have some stem tissue attached to each leaf. This aids in rooting and the production of plantlets. The last few central leaves can be left joined and treated as a stem cutting.

The remaining lower stem twelve months later has new plantlets developing.

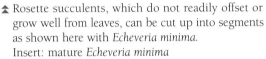

⤒ Rosette succulents, which do not readily offset or grow well from leaves, can be cut up into segments as shown here with *Echeveria minima.*
Insert: mature *Echeveria minima*

↘ Six months after cutting, the four rosette segments have established as independent plants which in turn can later provide offsets.

⤓ After eight years without any offsets this mature specimen of *Agave verschaffeltii* is sending up a tall flower stalk, after which it will die. By immediately cutting or sawing out the central stalk early and stopping any ensuing flower buds, the plant will survive and produce offsets the following year.

⤓ A solitary haworthia was cut evenly in two, dried for three weeks and then replanted separately. Both halves have now regrown. One has multiple heads, which can soon be cut away as cuttings.

Apical core drilling

While offsets will be produced on the great majority of stem and rosette succulents, the regularity and quantity produced is often very meagre. Many gardeners will have noted that once the growing tip at the top of the plant is damaged, branching will result. Propagators have several ways to mimic this natural process in order to produce more branching. The easiest way is to cut off the growing tip but this does not work well with all succulents. An alternative method is to use a drill to destroy the apical growth bud. An extra long 8 mm drill bit is recommended. With cactus and euphorbias 40 mm is an adequate depth, for aloes and agaves the drill bit needs to go deeper. The advantage of using a drill instead of trying to cut out the growing tip is that there is less damage to the leaves. The less leaf damage, the more offsets that will be produced. Plants drilled in this way react in two ways. If the growing tip has been destroyed the plant will produce copious offsets. If the drill missed or only damaged the growing tip, the plant will continue to grow from the top with some damage to the new leaves. If this occurs, the drilling procedure should be repeated.

Any deliberate damage of this nature to the apex of a succulent can leave a sizeable hole or depression. Avoid watering from the top and try to keep the hole dry. No chemicals or sealants are needed.

⤒ This *Euphorbia horrida* seedling remained solitary until its growing point was destroyed using a drill. While it could not grow a new tip, it has produced numerous offsets and will continue to do so for many years. When drilling out euphorbias always wear gloves and eye protection as the sap sprayed out by the turning drill is likely to be dangerous.

⤓ This rare *Agave pumila* was drilled twelve months earlier and has now produced several offsets. As the larger ones are removed, the smaller ones will replace them. Such a plant can produce dozens more over the following years, before slowly dying. Insert: A ten year old *Agave pumila*.

⤒ *Echinocactus grusonii*, the golden barrel cactus, grows as a solitary plant for thiry years or more. Here, a five years old specimen is drilled to destroy the growing apex. This is akin to pinching out the growing tip of garden plants. The only difference is that a drill is the only way to get down beneath the spines.

⤒ This 300 mm juvenile *E. grusonii* was drilled one year earlier and as a result has numerous offsets developing. If the offsets are not removed it will grow into a highly prized multiheaded specimen.

⤓ Drilling out the central growing point is a way of speeding up the development of offsets on plants that rarely, if ever, produce them. This *Agave filifera* f. *compacta*. will now produce numerous offsets in the coming months.

⤓ Twelve months later (from left). These new rosettes are being removed from the parent plant using a forceful lever action. Treat these as stem cuttings.

Grafting

Traditionally, grafting was used on fruit trees. Small branches from an exceptional tree were inserted into branches of other unremarkable trees that were similar but faster growing. Through experimentation, it was found that small buds or shoots could also be used and this is how most commercial grafting of horticultural crops is carried out today.

The procedure for grafting cactus is well covered in most other cactus oriented books. Rather than repeat the same information, we will focus on general succulent grafting as this not only applies to a broader range of succulents but also includes most cactus. While grafting itself may be considered advanced or difficult, this procedure can take many forms. Grafting is best done during late spring and summer unless additional warmth and heat is provided.

Grafting consists of two phases, the quick and precise graft procedure itself and a period of prolonged aftercare when the graft melds itself on to the rootstock. The grafting of succulents is best done on a clean, well lit bench. A piece of the desired plant is quickly and cleanly cut and inserted or bound to a cut surface on a hardier and vigorous related plant. It is important to make a single, even cut and avoid any sawing motion which would create an uneven surface. The grafting procedure is best done indoors and out of the sun, wind and too dry an atmosphere.

After-graft care should prevent the root stock from shooting out new growth. Pinch shoots out as soon as they appear.

⬧ Adeniums can be grafted on to oleander or frangipani seedling rootstocks. The graft consists of a young *Adenium obesum* seedling which has its severed upper stem cut into a v-shaped wedge. The lower portion is a frangipani seedling which has had its leaves removed (see insert) and its top 20 mm cut off and discarded. The remaining stem is cut into a cleft. The stem of the adenium is gently wedged within seconds of the cut into the cleft and usually tied firmly with thread.

⬧ After three weeks, the graft will have joined and the thread can be removed. Remove any new rootstock shoots as soon as they appear.

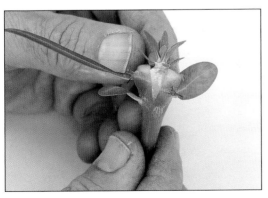

Grafting cactus

The brightly coloured cactus often sold in garden centres are all grafted on to a fast growing vigorous green rootstock (usually a hylocereus). Almost any cactus can be grafted on to any other cactus species. Generally, smaller, flatter, slower growing species are chosen to graft on to any fast growing taller types. Popular grafting stock is usually very hardy with few spines. This makes the process of grafting and aftercare a lot easier. Hylocereus, trichocereus and *Myrtillocactus geometrizans* are common rootstocks. For grafting seedlings use pereskiopsis as a rootstock.

It is advisable for fast growing grafts to be regrafted every few years. This is important for three main reasons:
1. The graft on top may outgrow its stem in size and fall over or break.
2. The graft grows much larger in size than the base. If this happens, the rootstock cannot feed or water the graft sufficiently.
3. Some rootstocks lose their green colour and eventually become corky or woody.

For further information on grafting, refer to the recommended reading list on page 109.

➤ Grafting is a specialised technique most commonly used by cactus growers to speed up growth of slower growing or rare offsets and seedlings. There are a number of techniques. The one shown here is a wedge graft, used to join *Pachypodium brevicaule* on to the hardier *P. lamerei*. Many general cactus related books (see page 109) have details of other grafting techniques.

Micro-propagation

As technology has advanced, so has the ability to be more precise and successful with smaller and smaller pieces of plant tissue. Once a whole stem or branch of a plant was required to produce an exact replica of the parent plant. Later, stems and flower stalks and finally only a stem bud, often no larger than a match head, were able to produce completely new plants. In most plants, trees and shrubs there are junctions along the stems or branches where new growths of flowers, leaves or new stems are formed. Generally these lie where stems meet leaves or other stems. These junctions contain the meristem tissue. Another way of interpreting the meristem is to understand that there are very specific small areas of tissue on all plants, which are capable of growing all the major new functioning parts a plant needs to survive. To propagate new plants from small slices of stem tissue, we need to have the meristem attached. The smaller the cutting, the more difficult the procedure is. Micro-propagation of succulents calls for sterilised precision tools to cut away meristems and maintain them in sterile environments, where they can be treated with growth hormones and other chemicals to induce the tissue to produce roots, shoots and leaves.

Micro-propagation has the great advantage of being able to produce thousands of plants from only a few pieces of meristem tissue within months and is now used to produce some of the slower growing and traditionally difficult-to-propagate succulents. One example is *Aloe polyphylla* which until recently was rare and expensive. Normally, a single juvenile specimen some 100 mm

⬆ These 150 mm specimens of the once very rare and much sought after *Aloe polyphylla* were tender, and grass-like plantlets in a flask only twelve months earlier.

in diameter would be five to ten years away from being able to reproduce via seeds. With micro-propagation, an immature specimen can be cut up to expose the meristem tissues at the base of the leaves. Within twelve months these will be able to produce thousands of small *Aloe polyphylla* plantlets ready for potting up.

The simplest form of micropropagation is the auxillary shoot method using seeds. Sterilised seeds are grown in sealed test tubes on nutrient agar until they are a manageable size. The roots are removed (in a sterile environment) and the plantlet is recultured on nutrient agar containing growth hormones which induce prolific offsetting. When large enough, the clump of offsets can be divided into individual plantlets. Hardier types such as agaves and aloes can be rooted as for normal cuttings, others require another stage to allow plantlets to produce roots in a sterile environment.

For further information about micro-propagation see the references on page 109.

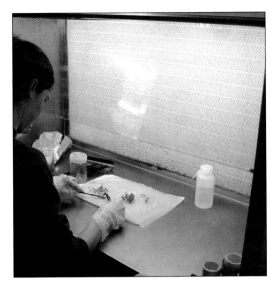

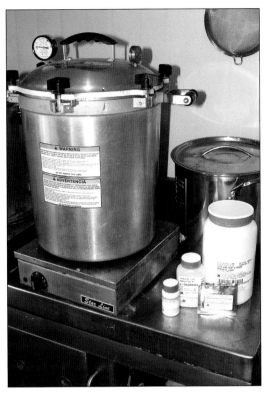

▲ While most laboratories are very high tech and expensive, they need not be. Here a laboratory technician works with delicate detail in a sterile environment. An airflow cabinet blows sterilised air over the work area, protecting it from infection.

▲ A commercial pressure cooker is used to sterilise equipment. All the chemicals required for micro-propagation are available from commercial suppliers.

▼ These three jars show growth rates. The far left jar is newly planted, the one in the hand is three months old and ready to be planted out.

▼ In sterile, sealed containers like this, plants are raised in a jelly-like nutrient solution.

Pests and diseases

During propagation there are a range of pests, diseases and other related problems that can arise. This applies especially when raising seed. Prevention is always preferable to treatment.

A clean work environment, clean tools and equipment and above all clean, healthy plant material to work with, will reduce pest and disease problems. Unfortunately, unless a sterile environment is available, as with micro-propagation in a laboratory, the likelihood is that there will always be some pests and diseases that need to be controlled.

Fungus infections are often a serious problem in raising seeds. The most common of these is called 'damping off'. In very humid environments, which are ideal for raising seeds, seedlings lose their green colour, turn greyish and then collapse inwards. Rather than decreasing the water supply, most growers quickly apply fungicides as soon as the problem appears. Some experienced growers use fungicides as a precaution every week or two with the watering, irrespective of any visible symptoms. If diseases or fungi are left unchecked they usually sweep from one plant to the whole tray, and can kill everything in a few short weeks.

Moss and liverworts can be a problem that often does not show itself until about six months after seedlings are sown. Remove where possible as they can smother tiny seedlings. Algae can also cover the surface of potting mixes, sometimes forming a crust, which when dry, contracts and damages seedlings. Use an algicide to prevent this.

Weeds are often a serious problem in homemade potting mixes. Commercial mixes are sterile and weed-free to start with but can quickly become infected with weed seeds coming in from elsewhere.

Sciarid flies and their larvae are a major insect pest of cactus seedlings but can also infect other succulents. The larvae of the sciarid fly generally eat fungus and dead or rotting organic matter in the potting mix. They also attack young seedlings, especially if damaged. Sciarid flies love humid, damp environments and are very tiny, mostly going unnoticed. Be vigilant and use an appropriate insecticide.

Snails are occasionally a problem. Sprinkle snail bait. For more detailed information on snails, mealy bugs and other important succulent pests, see our previous book in the series, *Succulents: Care and Health*.

Diseases and viruses

Once again, hygiene and prevention are always preferable. Use clean tools to take cuttings and every time you finish cutting from one plant, dip the cutting end of the blade into bleach or methylated spirits to sterilise, then dry. This prevents plant sap from one plant being transferred and contaminating the next plant that is cut. Viruses are very easily transferred from cut to cut and one sick plant can infect all of your propagation work. It may be months or the following year before blotchy, poor or weak growth develops. At this point there is no treatment for virus attack other than isolating infected plants and throwing them in the bin. Do not compost them. Infected plants never fully recover and will remain a source of infection to others.

⬆ This *Echeveria 'Black Prince'* plant is blotchy, weak and slow growing, which indicates a viral infection. Often a plant can be infected without showing any symptoms and remain seemingly healthy for a year or two before being overcome.

⬆ This picture was full of succulent seedlings only days before. Sciarid flies are fast moving, breed quickly and have larvae which attack and eat seedlings as well as helping to spread disease. Insert: Mature sciarid fly (enlarged five times).

⬇ This cactus seedling tray has become infected with a soil fungus which has killed many of the plants. The best solution is to remove the healthy seedlings and transplant them into sterile potting mix. Discard any that show signs of damage as these will infect the healthy seedlings.

⬇ This seedling tray has become infested with three species of weeds, all of which have explosive-type fruit which can shoot out seeds several metres. Such weeds can quickly infest seedling trays and pots and will smother small plants.

Seed raising

Seed production, collection and storage

While a few succulents are easy, multiplying most via seed is more involved and time critical than reproducing from offsets, cuttings, divisions and leaves. For many species of cactus, caudiciforms and mesembs, seeds are the most practical and most often used method of multiplication.

An educational and fun way to obtain succulent seeds is to harvest them from your own plants. The ability of plants to produce seeds will depend on factors such as maturity and genetic compatibility as well as whether cross-pollination (with a second plant) may be required, or whether it is self-fertile, in which case only one plant is required. If a plant does not produce seeds naturally, then assisted pollination will be required along with the need to identify male and female parts of a flower. The male flower part consists of lots of tiny stalks holding powdery yellow pollen. A central receiving platform (usually the tip of a thicker central rod in most flowers) is the female part of a flower. Assisted pollination consists of manually transferring pollen to the female parts. This is usually done by gently collecting and transferring pollen with a small paint brush (see photo).

Generally, flowering plants have both male and female parts in every flower; but, not all do. A minority are either male or female plants. Of these, only the flowering

⌃ Euphorbia flowers, male (left) and female (right)

⌃ These euphorbia fruit only develop on plants with female flower parts. Each fruit contains up to three seeds. When ripe the fruit explodes.

⌄ *Pleiospilos nellii* (red form shown here) are best raised from seeds. To obtain seeds, this plans was cross-pollinated with another using an artists brush. Insert: Four week old seedlings.

plants that have female parts can ever produce seeds. A male plant is still required to provide the necessary pollen for the flower to set seed on the female flowers.

Species which have male and female-only plants include adenias and some euphorbias such as the popular *E. obesa*. If no natural insect pollinator is present, a simple transfer of pollen (usually done with a small brush from the male flower to the female flower, will result in fertilisation and the production of a seed bearing fruit. In some cases, pollen must be exchanged between different plants (cross-pollination) even if the flowers are complete (having both male and female parts present). While it may be seen as a simple matter to exchange pollen between two plants, this will only produce fertilisation if the plants are genetically different, meaning that the parent plants were themselves produced from seeds or from different clones (selected types).

Plants which are produced from cuttings from the same parent, are genetically identical, so any attempt at seed production between such plants will fail (unless they are self-fertile). It is not easy to determine if succulents are genetically identical unless you have taken the cuttings yourself or you can verify the source as different.

Once pollination has occurred, the fruit will swell and become ripe. This can take from several weeks to six months and is usually recognised as being complete when the fruit changes colour, splits open or dries out. Ripe seeds are usually black or dark brown in colour. It is best to dry ripe seeds since the optimum time of sowing (late spring) is usually not when the seeds become ripe (usually summer or autumn).

(continued)

▲ Some cactus species are self-fertile and will produce fruit with viable seeds without cross-pollination by another plant. Fruit is ripe when the seeds inside them turn black (as above). Seeds can be squeezed out onto paper, then dried, stored and planted the following spring.

▼ Seeds can be separated from sticky, sugary fruit pulp by soaking the crushed fruit in water. Clean seeds will sink to the bottom. Hollow or dead seeds will float to the top.

⏶ Once ripe, many fruit split open, as with this *Aloe longistyla*. Seeds need to be collected before they are blown out or become wet from rain and dew. *Aloe longistyla* ripens in the early summer and can be sown immediately or can be stored for later sowing.

⏷ Echeverias and their related genera have small, five-segmented fruit which shed seeds when fully dry. The seeds are very small and almost dust-like. Dried fruit like these need to have the seeds separated from the chaff before they are sown or stored in packets. Crush them and use a sieve to separate as much as possible.

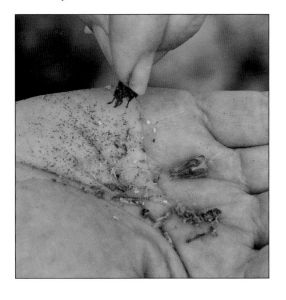

Setting seed on euphorbias is quite easy, but harvesting the seeds when ripe can be tricky. When ripe, each seed pod explodes open, throwing the seeds up to a metre or more away. It is not a good idea to pick unripe fruit early; rather, use a small net, stocking or sock to cover the areas with fruit. Set a tray or dish below the pot to catch the seeds that fall.

When seeds are harvested, they will need to be stored until sowing, preferably in small paper bags. Many succulent seeds can be stored for years, but only if certain conditions are met. Dampness and high temperatures are the enemy of seed in storage. The kitchen is a particularly poor place to store seed packets as the humidity from cooking will easily be absorbed by the seeds, thus reducing their viability. Keeping seeds cool is relatively easy if they are refrigerated, but make sure the seed packets are in a glass container with a metal lid as this will make them totally impervious to moisture in the refrigerator. Storing in a glass jar is also recommended if keeping seeds elsewhere in the house. Avoid keeping seeds just in loose paper packets as these will absorb moisture from the air. Over time, even small plastic zip-lock bags will absorb moisture. Rather, put all the paper or plastic seed packets into a large glass jar. Reducing the internal moisture is another good way of extending long term viability. Silica gel, a moisture absorbing rock-like substance, is used to remove humidity. A layer of active silica gel (this has a blue colour) at the bottom of a large glass jar will remove moisture. Silica gel can be reconditioned in a microwave. This will dry out the absorbed water, quickly turning it from pink back to bright blue as it is dried.

Sourcing seeds

Seeds are usually obtained either by collecting or purchasing them from a seed supplier. It is surprisingly easy to collect succulent seeds from your own plants. If you do not have your own plants to start with, visit friends and growers of succulents, who may share their seeds with you. Many gardens with succulents such as aloes and echeverias produce plentiful seeds every year that is often not wanted by its owners. You may wish to exchange seeds or buy it for a very small fee, if any at all. Your local botanic gardens support group may also be able to help with seeds. Local cactus and succulent societies are also a great way to contact like-minded people who may be interested in selling or exchanging succulent seeds.

Supermarkets only stock seeds of common annuals such as portulaca and Livingstone daisies. Many seed merchants have succulent seeds for sale, and often have a catalogue of their range. Succulent types such as agaves, aloes, lithops and some assorted or mixed cactus seeds are commonly available.

Many countries have specialist seed suppliers who sell nothing but succulent seeds. These specialists usually have the best selection. The prices for seeds purchased in quantity is very cheap compared to other commercial sources. One possible drawback is that some of the seeds may not be fresh.

The internet is a great place to start looking (see page 109) for seed suppliers, but shipments of seeds across international borders are restricted to varying degrees so enquire at your department of agriculture and/or customs and quarantine for further details as to any inspection fees and permits which may be required. A far quicker and cheaper option (yet more limited in selection) is to order seeds through suppliers based within your own country.

❥ Plastic bags should only be used for seeds that are completely dry. Seeds that may look dry are often still damp inside and eventually rot if stored prematurely in plastic bags.

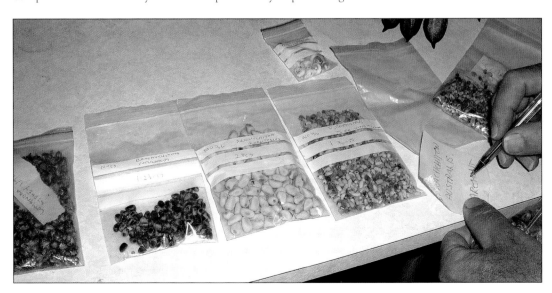

Propagating adeniums and pachypodiums

These two succulent genera are best raised from seeds, but getting seeds from your own plants is not a simple process. The flowers of most of the species in the *Apocynaceae* family have a complex structure which requires a special technique for hand pollination. In nature, the flowers are pollinated by moths, particularly those with a long proboscis which can reach down the long flower tube. The insects are only after the nectar at the bottom of the flower tube but in order to reach this they need to move their mouth part past the pollen and the stigma (female organ which the pollen needs to reach in order for pollination to take place). For hand pollination, it is best to mimic the action of a moth's proboscis as shown in the photograph. Monofilament fishing line can be used, as can a stiff hair such as horsetail. The fibre is carefully inserted into the end of the flower tube (see photo) and then withdrawn with a twisting action. Some pollen will stick near the tip of the fibre. This needs to be inserted into another flower using the same technique. Hopefully some of the pollen will stick to the female structures when withdrawn and will then develop into a fruit containing seeds. With most pachypodiums and adeniums, cross-pollination is required, but if you only have one plant flowering, it is worth giving a few flowers a try because some plants are self-fertile.

Fruit which develops need to be covered or secured so that the seeds are not blown away as the ripe fruit splits.

▲ *Pachypodium succulentum* form *griquensis* with a pollinating hair being inserted down the narrow flower tube. This species has very narrow flower tubes and it is not possible to look into the flower to check on the technique. Note the developing fruit behind the flower from a previous pollination.

▼ This flower of a *Pachypodium namaquanum* hybrid has been partially cut away to show the reproductive cone and some of the five slits through which the hair needs to be inserted. Using a twisting motion, it should be withdrawn so that it comes out from the top of the cone where the pollen is located. Flowers cut or torn open for easier access will not be as successful as keeping the flower whole.

⬘ *Adenium obesum* flowers. The previously pollinated horizontal flower has been removed from the ovary (blue arrow). The yellow arrow points to the 'cage' which sits above the ovary and contains the pollen in its upper portion. The stigma (which connects to the ovary) is in the lower section of the cage.

⬘ A nearly ripe *Adenium obesum* fruit. In this case, only one of the 'horns' was pollinated. This fruit should contain about sixty seeds.

⬙ *Pachypodium bispinosum* flower and fruit. The flower of this species is very easy to pollinate because it has an open floral tube, allowing the procedure to be seen. The fruit (which do not change colour when ripe) is almost ready to split and will need to be covered or taped shut to keep the seeds from blowing away.
Insert: A section of drinking straw, cut open along its length, is used to hold the fruit closed. Fruit can also be covered with netting or the like but we find that a straw is the easiest to use on small fruit.

⬙ *Pachypodium namaquanum* fruit. By the time the fruit is ripe the leaves have normally all been shed. Each fruit contains about thirty seeds which are best sown immediately.
Insert: Plant in leaf.

Sowing large seeds

plant name	best season for sowing	time before handling	height + width after one year	height + width after five years	notes
Adansonia gibbosa	early summer	3 months	120 x 80 mm	2 x 1 m	5, 8, 9
Adenia glauca	early summer	3 months	120 x 80 mm	1 x 1 m	8, 9
Adenium obesum	early summer	3 months	120 x 80 mm	1 x 1 m	9
Agave attenuata	spring	6 months	120 x 120 mm	0.5 x 0.5 m	2, 6
Agave filifera	spring	6 months	40 x 60 mm	0.4 x 0.6 m	2, 6
Agave parrasana	spring	6 months	40 x 60 mm	0.4 x 0.4 m	2
Agave parryi	spring	6 months	40 x 60 mm	0.4 x 0.5 m	2
Agave stricta	spring	6 months	70 x 80 mm	0.5 x 0.6 m	2
Agave victoriae-reginae	spring	6 months	30 x 50 mm	0.2 x 0.4 m	2
Aloe bainesii	early spring	4 months	150 x 70 mm	2 x 1 m	1
Aloe deltoideodonta	early spring	4 months	30 x 40 mm	0.1 x 0.2 m	1, 6
Aloe ferox	early spring	4 months	80 x 70 mm	1 x 1 m	1
Aloe karasbergensis	early spring	4 months	50 x 70 mm	0.2 x 0.3 m	1
Aloe marlothii	early spring	4 months	80 x 70 mm	1 x 0.9 m	1
Aloe pillansii	late spring	4 months	40 x 60 mm	0.2 x 0.1 mm	1
Aloe plicatilis	early spring	4 months	140 x 90 mm	1 x 1 m	1, 10
Aloe polyphylla	early spring	4 months	40 x 50 mm	0.3 x 0.6 m	1, 8, 10
Beaucarnea recurvata	spring	6 months	140 x 80 mm	1 x 0.6 m	2
Beschorneria yuccoides	spring	4 months	70 x 80 mm	1 x 1.5 m	
Brachychiton rupestris	late spring	3 months	120 x 80 mm	2 x 1 m	5, 8
Cereus peruvianus	spring	12 months	30 x 10 mm	2 x 0.1 m	3, 6, 7
Chorisia speciosa	late spring	3 months	120 x 80 mm	3 x 3 m	9
Dasylirion wheeleri	early spring	10 months	80 x 30 mm	0.6 x 0.6 m	
Dioscorea elephantipes	early spring	6 months	n/a	n/a	1, 8, 10
Dracaena draco	late spring	4 months	120 x 120 mm	1.5 x 1 m	5, 8
Euphorbia bupleurifolia	spring	3 months	20 x 100 mm	0.1 x 0.1 m	
Euphorbia caput-medusae	spring	6 months	60 x 30 mm	.01 x 1 m	10
Euphorbia enopla	spring	6 months	40 x 20 mm	0.2 x 0.2 m	6
Euphorbia grandialata	spring	6 months	40 x 20 mm	1.5 x 1.5 m	
Euphorbia rigida	early spring	3 months	60 x 60 mm	0.4 x 0.9 m	
Fockea edulis	late spring	4 months	n/a	n/a	
Hesperaloe parviflora	spring	6 months	60 x 30 mm	0.4 x 0.4 m	
Nolina gracilis	spring	6 months	120 x 80 mm	1.5 x 1 m	
Opuntia species	late spring	10 months	variable	variable	2, 4, 6, 8
Oreocereus celcianus	late spring	12 months	20 x 10 mm	1 x 0.1 m	6, 7
Pachypodium lamerei	early summer	3 months	80 x 80 mm	1.5 x 0.6 m	9
Pachypodium rosulatum	early summer	3 months	70 x 20 mm	0.3 x 0.2 m	9
Yucca brevifolia	spring	6 months	100 x 70 mm	0.6 x 0.2 m	
Yucca rostrata	spring	6 months	110 x 80 mm	0.6 x 0.6 m	
Yucca whipplei	spring	6 months	110 x 80 mm	0.6 x 0.6 m	

Sowing large seeds

Large seeds of succulents are considered by us to be match-head size or larger (3 mm+). Large seeds are generally slower to germinate than small seeds. In some cases, seeds can take weeks or months to germinate, but it is not uncommon for a few late starters in a seed tray to germinate up to a year after sowing. As a general rule, the larger the seed and the thicker the seed coat, the longer it will take to germinate. It is a good idea to soak large seeds in warm water overnight before planting as this reduces normal germination time by at least half. Seeds need to be slightly buried. Either push the seeds into the potting mix (see photo below) or lie them on to the surface and cover with more potting mix or sand, so that they are fully buried. It is important not to let the seeds dry out after planting.

To speed up germination of thick, hard seeds, growers should abrade the seeds, using sand paper or a file. The object is to wear away a small portion of the seed coat and speed up the absorption of water. An extension of this form of treatment is the cracking, chipping or cutting away of part of the hard seed casing with a sharp knife or saw blade. Take care not to damage any of the white inner seed which is very delicate. Abrading the seed coat is done before soaking in warm water. A number of chemicals have been shown to increase the germination of many succulent seeds (see page 109 for a reference).

Large seeds produce large seedlings, so do not plant them too close together. If you have several seeds of a plant and only really want one good one to grow, then why not plant all of them in a moderate-sized pot and as they come up you can select the most healthy and vigorous one and weed out the weaker ones around it.

Comments for table, page 56

1: Sprinkle soil over seeds to hold down.
2: Bury slightly.
3: Sprinkle seeds on to soil, do not cover.
4: Bury well into soil.
5: Soak twelve hours in warm water before sowing.
6: Smallish seeds.
7: Cactus species (see page 62).
8: Irregular germination.
9: Minimum temperature of 20°C.
10: Maximum temperature of 20°C.

▼ Larger seeds can be pushed to the correct depth (about twice their diameter) by using a pencil. The holes can be filled with sand. Recording the number of seeds planted and how many germinate will give a good indication of the viability of the seeds.

Sowing small seeds

plant name	best season for sowing	time before handling	height + width after one year	height + width after five years	notes
Aeonium nobile	early autumn	6 months	70 x 100 mm	300 x 300 mm	2, 10
Cheiridopsis species	spring + autumn	3 months	50 x 50 mm	60 x 100 mm	10
Dorotheanthus bellidoniformis	autumn-winter	1 month	n/a	n/a	
Dudleya brittonii	autumn-winter	6 months	40 x 60 mm	180 x 300 mm	3, 6, 10
Echeveria 'Blue Curl's	spring	6 months	60 x 80 mm	160 x 220 mm	5, 9
Echeveria elegans	spring	4 months	40 x 60 mm	60 x 200 mm	
Echeveria frilly hybrids	spring	6 months	60 x 80 mm	160 x 220 mm	5, 9
Echeveria imbricata	spring	6 months	50 x 100 mm	120 x 250 mm	
Echeveria laui	spring-summer	6 months	20 x 30 mm	50 x 100 mm	1, 6, 9
Echeveria minima	spring-summer	6 months	20 x 20 mm	40 x 50 mm	9
Echeveria tolimanensis	spring-summer	6 months	30 x 30 mm	50 x 70 mm	9
Graptopetalum bellum	spring + autumn	6 months	20 x 30 mm	50 x 100 mm	6, 9
Greenovia aurea	autumn-winter	3 months	40 x 40 mm	100 x 150 mm	2, 3, 10
Haworthia fasciata	winter-spring	12 months	10 x 10 mm	100 x 100 mm	3
Haworthia retusa	winter	12 months	10 x 10 mm	40 x 100 mm	3
Haworthia tesselata	winter	12 months	10 x 10 mm	40 x 60 mm	3
Lithops optica f. *rubra*	spring + autumn	12 months	10 x 10 mm	20 x 30 mm	1, 6
Lithops lesliei	spring + autumn	12 months	10 x 10 mm	20 x 50 mm	1
Lithops aucampiae	spring + autumn	10 months	20 x 20 mm	30 x 60 mm	1
Orostachys iwarange	spring	6 months	80 x 80 mm	n/a	1, 3, 10
Pleiospilos simulans	spring + autumn	6 months	40 x 50 mm	50 x 120 mm	1
Portulaca grandiflora	spring	1 month	n/a	n/a	2, 3
Sempervivum tectorum	spring + autumn	6 months	30 x 40 mm	60 x 200 mm	3, 10

Notes for above table

1: Adult and flowering within three years.
2: Annual species.
3: Give extra shade in summer.
4: Bury seeds.
5: Prefers humidity.
6: A challenge, even for the experts.
7: Very prone to pests and diseases.
8: Minimum temperature 20°C.
9: Minimum temperature 15° C.
10: Maximum temperature 20°C.

Sowing small seeds

Small seeds of succulents vary in size from dust-like to coarse sand grains. The smaller the seeds, the more difficult it is to handle and sow.

If packets of seeds are opened outdoors be aware that even a small breeze (or a sneeze!) can blow them out of your hands. It is best to plant seeds on a calm day or alternatively plant them under cover. No pretreatment is required for most small succulent seeds before planting. Just lightly sprinkle the seeds on to the surface of your propagating potting mix. The type of propagation mix you use is not as important as having a topping of coarse washed river sand (or aquarium sand) on top of the propagating mix. When seeds are sprinkled over the surface and gently watered in, the seeds will trickle down among the larger grains of river sand, where they will get some shade as well as essential support as they begin to grow between the grains. If you have unsteady hands, or would like to have a more even seed distribution over your seedling tray, mix the dry seeds with half a cup of dry river sand. Then just sprinkle the sand out evenly as you would for the seeds alone. This method is highly recommended as it gives a more even spread of seedlings. Germination will usually appear in a few days or weeks, while stragglers may take months. For raising seedlings, see pages 60-63.

◀◀ A small amount of fine pre-washed and dried sand is mixed with tiny seeds before being sprinkled on to a seedling tray using a sheet of folded paper to pour with. This method distributes seeds evenly and leads to a better spread of seedlings.

The basics

Midspring, when temperatures are between 15°C and 25°C, is the best time to sow most succulents. Sow seeds in black plastic pots or trays that can hold at least a 40 mm depth of potting mix. All-purpose seed raising mix for general plants can be used, especially for the leafy or shrubby succulents. Any potting mix suitable for succulents can also be used. It is also good practice to sieve the potting mix if there are many large particles over 3 mm. Desert types, which are more compact in their stems, such as lithops, some euphorbias and all cactus, need a more porous mix. A twelve-month slow release all-purpose fertiliser may be mixed in before sowing. Add it at half the recommended rate on the label. Before sowing most succulent seeds, gently flatten or pat down the potting mix. When watering use only a soft, gentle spray to prevent splashing and the dislodging of any seeds.

Many growers cover newly planted succulent seeds with glass or plastic sheets which must be removed once germination occurs. A covering material is used to increase humidity and provide shade. Extra shade cloth may also be necessary during this period. The zip-lock bag process is an alternative to glass and plastic sheets (only recommended for cactus, see page 63).

Caring for succulent seedlings

The ideal conditions for raising most types of succulents (for cactus, see page 63) from seeds is a humid environment which is preferably out of direct sunlight, especially if summers are very hot and dry. Temperatures of 15-25°C are preferable. For the first two or three months seeds and seedlings need to be kept damp and never allowed to dry out even for a day. Water daily or more if need be. Once germinated, the larger the seed, the faster the seedling growth rate.

Shade cloth is often used to keep the sun off tender seedlings. This is slowly removed over the following three months. After one or two months the atmosphere should be made less humid. The potting mix and succulent roots still need to be kept slightly damp. Only water when the surface of the potting mix is starting to show signs of drying out. When seedlings are large enough to handle easily or have become crowded in the original seedling tray or pot, transplant them carefully. If possible, try not to disturb the roots. Dig the seedling out with potting mix still attached to the roots and repot without pressing in. Do this by making a hole in slightly damp potting mix and lowering the seedling root system into the hole. Close the hole but do not press the potting mix down. A little gentle shake or tapping of the pot may help settle the seedling in. Water in very lightly. The use of a watering can to apply a general fungicide is advisable but not essential. Small seedlings that grow very slowly may need to be retrayed into a fresh tray and mix, rather than be individually potted for another year. Once leafy succulent seedlings have five leaves they can be replanted, if the weather is still warm enough. To reach this stage may take three to six months from germination.

Many hobbyists raising succulent seedlings the first time may not want ten or twenty seedlings and yet each packet of seeds has no less. What do you do with so many seedlings if all the seeds germinate and only one or two are wanted? Plant all the seeds in a pot and keep only the fastest growers in the middle while gently weeding out the slower and weaker plants. The ones that remain in the pot will have had the least disturbance and the best chance of survival.

⩧ *Echeveria elegans* seedlings. The seeds pictured on page 52 were immediately sprinkled on to damp potting mix and watered daily. For the first few days a shade cloth covering was used, and subsequently only used on very hot days. The upper picture was taken six days after planting and the lower picture was taken three months later.

⏶ Seedlings (right) are slower growing than plantlets from leaf cuttings (left) until they have reached this size. At this stage the seedlings are as fast growing and easy to care for as plants grown from cuttings.

⏶ Seedlings of *Dracaena draco* being sorted out and repotted individually. The seeds were sown twelve months earlier.

⏷ These tall, leggy *Euphorbia obesa* seedlings grew when this pot was kept in too much shade. It was later moved to a better lit location, as shown by the more compact seedlings in the background which germinated later. Compare these seedlings to those on page 1 grown under more light.

Agave seedlings, (twice actual size) about three ⏷ weeks after sowing. Agave seedlings are very uniform in germination and growth. The empty seed coat often remains on the apex of the seedlings. Do not remove these as they will eventually fall off.

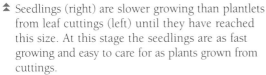

Sowing cactus seeds

genus	best season for sowing	time before handling	height + width after one year	height + width after five years	notes (see below)
Astrophytum	late spring	12 months	10 x 10 mm	50 x 50 mm	2, 4, 9
Carnegia	late spring	12 months	10 x 10 mm	100 x 70 mm	9
Cephalocereus	late spring	12 months	10 x 10 mm	50 x 30 mm	9
Cereus	spring	12 months	30 x 10 mm	2 x 0.1 m	1, 2, 3, 9
Cleistocactus	spring	12 months	20 x 10 mm	2 x 0.1 m	9
Copiapoa	early spring	12 months	10 x 10 mm	100 x 100 mm	9
Discocactus	late spring	12 months	110 x 10 mm	20 x 30 mm	5, 6, 8, 10
Echinocactus	late spring	12 months	110 x 10 mm	130 x 170 mm	9
Echinocereus	early spring	8 months	10 x 10 mm	variable	9
Epiphyllum hybrids	late spring	6 months	200 x 60 mm	1 x 1 m	1, 9
Epithelantha	late spring	12 months	110 x 10 mm	30 x 20 mm	9
Espostoa	late spring	12 months	110 x 10 mm	1 x 0.1 m	9
Ferocactus	late spring	12 months	10 x 10 mm	150 x 100 mm	4, 9
Gymnocalycium	spring	12 months	10 x 10 mm	30 x 80 mm	9
Mammillaria	spring	8 months	10 x 20 mm	50 x 200 mm	1, 3, 9
Mamillopsis	spring	12 months	10 x 10 mm	100 x 150 mm	9
Melocactus	late spring	10 months	10 x 10 mm	80 x 100 mm	1, 5, 8, 9
Myrtillocactus	late spring	10 months	20 x 10 mm	1 x 0.3 m	9
Notocactus	spring	12 months	10 x 10 mm	250 x 70 mm	9
Opuntia	late spring	10 months	variable	variable	2, 4, 6, 9
Oreocereus	late spring	12 months	20 x 10 mm	1 x 0.11 m	9
Parodia	spring	12 months	10 x 10 mm	variable	3, 9
Sclerocactus	autumn	12 months	10 x 10 mm.	50 x 30 mm	10
Uebelmannia	summer	12 months	10 x 10 mm.	50 x 30 mm	8, 9

Notes for above table

1: Recommended for beginners.
2: Bury slightly.
3: Extremely small seeds.
4: Irregular germination.
5: Prefers ongoing humidity.
6: A challenge even for experienced growers.
7: Soak seeds before sowing.
8: Minimum temperature 20°C.
9: Minimum temperature 15°C.
10: Maximum temperature 20°C.

Raising cactus from seeds

Raising cactus from seeds is not for the impatient. It can take up to a year for many cactus seedlings to reach the size of a pea. Cactus seedlings are more fragile than most succulents. Unlike other succulents, cactus seedlings can be kept covered in plastic and also be kept damp for several months. Other than this, sowing and germination advice is similar to the information for sowing and germinating succulents found on page 59.

By late autumn watering can almost cease until the next spring. In colder climates, watering of cactus seedlings may need to cease by early autumn, while in warmer or tropical climates watering may continue into and sometimes through winter.

A very practical way of raising cactus from seeds is to plant them in small pots or punnets. Water the seedlings well and then place the pots in a sealed zip-lock plastic bag. The bag will sweat and recycle most of the water the seedlings need. This is simple and easy as well as requiring the least amount of additional water and monitoring. The seedlings will take care of themselves. The bags can be left sealed for three months or more (aside from any necessary inspections).

◄◄ Seedlings of *Echinocactus grusonii* ('golden barrel') at three weeks, three months, five months and fourteen months. Well grown seedlings should not be elongated or excessively green.

Keep out of direct sun as this will cook the seedlings in the bag. Small numbers of cactus seedlings grown in pots and sealed in bags are easy to bring indoors to keep warm over winter and so continuing growth will occur in bright light.

If cactus seedlings are kept too wet, water-borne diseases occasionally set in. Watch for signs of fungus or disease (see pages 48 for more details).

Transplanting cactus seedlings is best done in the following spring. Dig out each seedling with its roots and replant in fresh potting mix in small pots. It is also common practice to retray them for one more year in a fresh tray and mix, planting in rows with even spacings, leaving approximately 20 mm between each plant. When replanting, make a hole in slightly damp potting mix and lower the seedling's roots into the hole. Then pour dry potting mix in around its base to fill all the spaces. Do not press or push in as this will damage roots. Handling cactus seedlings can be done without gloves. Most young cactus seedlings have soft spines which allow for easy, delicate handling with fingers. Hold the cactus seedling gently by its body and not by the roots.

Do not water in after transplanting. Watering can resume after one week. This drying time is needed to seal any wounds on the seedling. A general fungicidal spray is often used after the first watering, which can be a good soaking. Until a cactus seedling is two years old it will need some protection from direct summer sun, especially if temperatures regularly exceed 30°C.

Propagation by genus

Plants are grouped alphabetically by genus and we provide specific information relevant to their propagation. The most common method of propagation is described first.

Adenia

A genus of fifty succulent species of tropical and subtropical caudiciforms. The most common species are *A. glauca* and *A. spinosa*.

All adenias are best propagated from seeds. Cross-pollination is necessary as they are generally either only male or female plants. Pollination is best carried out with a small brush. Adenias will flower several times during a warm summer. Flowers are short lived so pollination must be undertaken as soon as both male and female flowers are open. Fruits develop quickly and ripen within four or five weeks. Each fruit contains 3-10 seeds. These usually germinate better when stored for a season. They are long lasting and will store for several years.

Seeds germinate quickly during the warmest months, but germination is often erratic, with some seeds germinating much later (up to twelve months later) than the earliest, which can pop up within ten days of sowing.

Adenias can be propagated from large stem cuttings (well below fresh green stems) taken during midsummer. Adenias can also be propagated from root cuttings (see page 38).

⮝ *Adenia spinosa* showing two nearly ripe fruits. Insert: Fully ripe fruit (actual size) split but retain their sticky covered seeds for months. This sticky dried pulp is best rubbed off before sowing.

⮟ One year old seedlings of *Adenia glauca* (left), *A. spinosa* and *A. repanda*. These are now ready to pot up; however, the tap roots should be cut to about half their length before potting up, especially if they are going into shallow pots, as shown.

Adenium

This genus contains about five species of tropical to subtropical caudiciforms (although this is still open to debate). *Adenium obesum* is by far the most common species and is mainly grown for its flowers, which come in a range of colours from pure white to intense crimson.

The common reddish flowered varieties are grown from seeds which germinate readily. Seedlings can flower within two years. Cross-pollination is usually required but some types are self-fertile. For pollination information, see page 54. The fruits are long and bean shaped and usually ripen in autumn but will sometimes carry over through winter, ripening only once the weather warms up again. The ripe seeds, which are attached to parachutes, float away on the slightest breeze.

In warm, humid areas, plants can be propagated from large stem cuttings, which can root quickly.

The fancy coloured or larger flowering adeniums, or those with variegated or coloured leaves, are generally reproduced by grafting on to the hardier seedlings of the more common *Adenium obesum* or on to oleander or even frangipani seedlings (see page 44).

Seeds of *Adenium obesum* are usually available from seed suppliers. Fresh seed is best as adenium seed is not viable for very long and should be planted as soon as possible, keeping in mind that they need warm to hot conditions to germinate and grow.

⬆ *Adenium swazicum* flowers, slightly smaller than actual size.

⬇ Seedlings of *Adenium swazicum* (left) and *A. obesum*. The smaller seedlings are about three months old, the larger ones about one year. Note how the tap-roots are twisted, indicating that the pot was not deep enough to allow for unrestricted growth.

Adromischus

A genus of miniature leaf succulents which can develop a small caudex when mature. There are at least twenty-eight species with hundreds of forms.

The easiest way to propagate most adromischus is from leaves which root well during spring and midautumn. Plantlets from leaf cuttings grow quickly, but only if the weather is not too hot as this slows down their growth. These plantlets benefit from afternoon shade, especially during summer.

Adromischus which develop clumps can also be divided in spring and autumn. This method is necessary for *A. phillipsiae,* which does not grow from leaves.

Adromischus can be grown from seeds but cross-pollination is necessary. The fruit is small and the seeds are shed easily once dry, so collect them as soon as the first seed pods open. For seed raising information, see page 59.

▲ *Adromischus phillipsiae* is best propagated from stem cuttings as it does not grow from leaves. The thicker the stem, the longer the callousing time required.

↖ Many adromischus eventually develop a sizeable caudex. Unfortunately they then begin to go into decline and need to be propagated and started again. From this plant it would be possible to take several stem cuttings as well as leaves.

⩢ A selection of adromischus grown from leaf cuttings. Plants from leaves will often flower (as several are doing here) when about a year old. To keep the plants growing, pinch off the flower stalks early.

Aeonium

A large genus containing thirty-six species and numerous garden hybrids. Almost all species are winter growing, shrub forming rosette succulents.

The shrubby species are easily propagated from stem cuttings taken just below each rosette. Roots form quickly from autumn through to spring. Growth and root formation will be severely inhibited by high summer temperatures.

Those few species which rarely offset and therefore remain as a single rosette, such as the popular *A. tabuliforme*, can be propagated by leaf cuttings which form roots and plantlets quickly during early autumn. Roots are usually produced from the leaves well before the plantlet forms. It is not necessary to plant leaves with roots immediately as they can survive for weeks lying about in air. Once the plantlets appear, they should be planted in damp potting mix. Other species of *Aeonium* can also be propagated by leaves, but not as easily as *A. tabuliforme*.

Aeoniums grow well but slowly from seeds. Some species are self-fertile, others are not. The seeds are dust-like and are best harvested in late spring just before the fruits naturally split and release the seeds. Fruit can be stored in a paper bag to fully ripen and then be sieved out later for sowing from autumn through to spring. For more information on raising small seeds, see page 59.

Aeoniums in the garden may set their own seeds and produce numerous seedlings if conditions are favourable. Careful selection of the most attractive or vigorous ones may produce rewarding new hybrids.

⚁ Most aeoniums in people's gardens are hybrids with dubious names and an untraceable history. This assortment of stem cuttings took only four weeks to establish an extensive root system. No callous time was necessary.

⚁ *Aeonium tabuliforme* is most commonly propagated from lower leaves which are peeled away carefully. It may be hard to do with an almost stemless plant, so by growing it for a few weeks in a very shady place it will stretch out, as seen on the left. Now even stem cuttings are possible.
Insert: *A. 'Velour'* (an *A. tabuliforme* hybrid) grown from a leaf.

Agave

There are over 100 species of agaves, ranging in size from miniatures to ones with a spread of 6 metres. All form rosettes. Most species produce rhizomes or offsets, while a few remain single.

Those species which produce rhizomes are the easiest to propagate. Dig up rhizomes once they develop a small offset with at least five leaves. By then, most will already have functioning roots. The species which develop clustering offsets around the stem are harder to propagate as the spines on the parent plant often make it difficult to get to the offsets underneath.

The least common agaves are those which produce few if any rhizomes or offsets. These can be forced to produce offsets using apical coring (see page 42) or can be grown from seeds (page 57). Agaves flower only once after which the main plant (but not the offsets) dies. Some species produce bulbils (see page 13) on the flowering stalk which can be removed once they begin to naturally drop. Flower stalks are generally only produced once plants are fully mature, which can take from seven to thirty-five or more years. Immature plants have been known to flower after becoming stressed from replanting or being excessively disturbed.

Many agave species are self-fertile. Harvest the seeds when the fruit turns brown and begins to split. Seeds are relatively large (2-4 mm) and are best sown in the warmest months. For seed raising information, see page 57.

Agave sap can cause skin irritation, wear gloves when handling plants.

⌃ The normal form of *Agave americana* (right), has many forms which are variegated, as seen on the left. Variegated agaves like these cannot be grown from seeds. They can only be multiplied from offsets.

⌄ *Agave attenuata* is spectacular when in flower, lasting for many months, after which the main plant slowly dies. The flower stalk may be up to 3 metres long with thousands of tiny flowers. Watch for either seeds or bulbils which usually follow.

Aloe

There are around 300 species of aloe which are quite diverse in size, growth habit and environmental requirements. Only a few dozen are commonly seen in gardens or in general succulent collections.

Most species produce offsets or branches which can be cut and treated as stem cuttings. Except for a very few winter growing species, stem cuttings or offsets are best taken during the warmer months. As a general rule, the smaller the species, the faster it will propagate. Small stem cuttings root best, as old or large stems can be very slow.

Those aloes that do not readily produce offsets need to be propagated from seeds. In general, aloes need cross-pollination for successful seed set. Pollination is easy and is often carried out by birds as they feed on the flower nectar. Bird pollination usually results in cross-species pollination, especially in gardens containing several different aloe species. The more aloes flowering at the same time, the higher the rate of hybridisation.

Aloe seeds germinate well but generally take longer than agaves and other related genera. No pretreatment is necessary. Most aloe seeds keep well in storage for several years.

Rare and slower growing species that seldom produce offsets or seeds can be cored (see page 42) to force offsets to be produced.

Micro-propagation is now used by the nursery industry to produce some of the rarer species, such as *Aloe polyphylla*.

⯅ Aloes flower regularly each year and are visited by nectar feeding birds that inadvertently pollinate them. As a result, fruit and seeds are commonly available on garden grown plants.

⯆ *Aloe mitriformis* offsets being cut away from the base of a mature plant. The smaller offsets will establish more quickly than the larger offsets, which are deliberately not being cut for this reason.

Anacampseros

A genus of about fifty miniature species. There has been a recent taxonomic revision of this genus, we refer to the older grouping which includes all known species.

Most species can be propagated from stem cuttings (see page 18) which are best taken during spring or early autumn. The white-leafed species, sometimes referred to as the scale-leafed types because of their appearance, are generally very difficult to grow from cuttings.

All anacampseros species flower freely and can be propagated from seeds. Many will reach flowering size within twelve months. Anacampseros flowers are often self-pollinating without actually opening and will set abundant seeds in this manner. If flowers open, it is in late afternoon, especially on hot summer days. Some species can become a nuisance in a pot collection because they set seeds throughout the summer, often germinating in neighbouring pots and becoming weeds. The less common species need to be cross-pollinated. The fruits are small and when dry shed seeds freely, so they need to be harvested quickly. Fruits usually take only three weeks to mature. Seeds germinate and grow quickly and are best sown in spring. Treat them as for small seeds, page 59.

⬆ *Anacampseros alstonii* is a miniature caudex forming species which can only be grown from seeds. Insert: A ripe fruit on *A. papyracea*, one of the scale-leafed types, at about actual size. Seeds are easily shed from ripe fruit so harvest carefully to avoid losing seeds. These types of anacampseros cannot be grown easily from cuttings.

⬇ A selection of anacampseros. Note the self-sown seedlings, some of which were also coming up in surrounding pots amd becoming weedy.

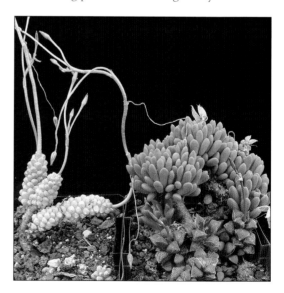

Beaucarnea
(including *Calibanus*, *Nolina* and *Dasylirion*)

These closely related genera contain woody stemmed plants with grass-like foliage. The most sought after are the larger growing species which form stout stems or which have neat and tidy rosette leaf arrangements.

Large lower stem cuttings are possible on a few species, but these may be difficult to establish.

All are generally grown from seeds as they very rarely offset. Flowers are usually male or female and on separate plants. Some species, such as *Calibanus hookeri*, will flower at around six or seven years of age if grown quickly, while others take decades to flower. During their first year or two most seedlings look like a coarse grass. These generally grow quickly and most develop an interesting size and character within two or three years. For more information on seed raising see page 57.

⬆ *Beaucarnea stricta* (left) and *Beaucarnea recurvata* (syn. *Nolina recurvata*). Both plants were seed grown. The back plant reached maturity at 1.5 metres in height and has flowered and set thousands of seeds.

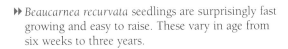

▸▸ *Beaucarnea recurvata* seedlings are surprisingly fast growing and easy to raise. These vary in age from six weeks to three years.

Bromeliads
(including *Abromeitiella*, *Deuterochonia*, *Dyckia* and *Hechtia*)

There are dozens of terrestrial species of bromeliads which have thick, succulent leaves and are often grown by succulent collectors.

Terrestrial bromeliads are usually propagated from offsets. Most of the terrestrial broms produce offsets which are held closely to the parent plant. Removal generally requires considerable force and care, especially with the more spiny species. Offsetting usually occurs when plants flower but many species will develop one or two offsets even when quite young. Offsets are best removed once they are twelve months old. Smaller offsets which do not have their own roots will need to be treated as cuttings (page 34).

Abromeitiella species grow as tight clumping plants with small, equal sized rosettes. Clumps can be cut or divided during the warmest months. Clumps of rosettes often have branches which have already developed roots and these can be immediately potted up and watered. Single rosettes taken as cuttings are difficult to root.

All species can be grown from seeds. Cross-pollination will usually be necessary for fruit set. Fruits split open when dry, but will retain seeds for some time. For seed raising information, see page 59.

⊼ *Abromeitiella* species form dense clumps of even sized rosettes. The best way to propagate them is to cut or tear apart larger clumps. Note that many of the divisions already have roots and so can be potted up immediately.

⊽ Dyckias look superb as single rosettes but as they multiply they lose some of their visual appeal. Removal of large offsets or dividing clumps of spiny ones like this becomes increasingly harder as crowded rosettes interlock. Removal of offsets early when they are small is easy. They establish more readily than mature sized offsets.
Insert: Removing this small offset will encourage more to develop.

Bulbs
(including *Haemanthus, Boophane, Ornithogallum, Massonia* and *Scilla*)

Several genera of bulbs are often grown by succulent collectors because they have very succulent leaves and tolerate the same growing conditions as most succulents. The most commonly grown species are *Haemanthus concinnus* and *H. albiflos*.

Most of the bulb species eventually form clumps which can be divided (see page 14). This is best done just before the new season's growth appears.

Some of the bulbs produce smaller offset bulbs. The larger of these can be peeled away and grown as cuttings. Some will have roots, and those that do not will grow quickly if treated as cuttings.

The seeds of succulent leafed bulbs can be either large and fleshy (*Haemanthus* and *Boophane*) or smaller and dry. The former need to be cross-pollinated. Once the fleshy fruits, which contain a single large seed are ripe, they need to be harvested immediately and planted. Seeds do not store for very long and will often grow a root within weeks of harvest, whether planted or stored.

Some bulb species are self-fertile, but most require cross-pollination. Sow the seeds in autumn as they are mostly winter growers.

⤒ *Massonia pustulata*, a succulent desert bulb that is often grown by cactus and succulent collectors. It flowers readily in early winter. Most plants are self-fertile and produce abundant and easy to harvest seeds.
Insert: A dormant *Massonia* bulb in summer.

⤓ Three month old seedlings of *Massonia pustulata*.

Ceropegia

There are at least 100 species of ceropegias.
Most are viny climbers which twist up and
around other tall growing plants to gain support and access to sunlight. Some species are
shrubs, a small group are creepers, while
other species produce a tuber from which
annual growth is produced. Most ceropegias
can be easily propagated from stem cuttings
(150-200 mm long) taken during the warmer
months. The thinner stemmed types can be
planted immediately and kept in a humid
atmosphere until the first roots are produced.
They can then be grown in a drier place like
other succulents. Thicker stem cuttings may
need a few weeks to callous.

Many ceropegias flower heavily, producing
hundreds of blooms during summer. Ceropegia
flowers require specialised pollination techniques and cannot be pollinated using a
brush or a hair-like filament. Sometimes
small flies pollinate flowers, producing two
horn-like fruit. These split open when ripe,
releasing seeds for the wind to distribute.
Fresh seeds germinates well and can be
treated as described on page 57.

⬆ Ceropegia cuttings just starting to grow new roots.
These can now be planted into damp potting mix.
It is easier to manage thin cuttings such as these in
a bundle, held together by a rubber band. Once
the cuttings show new growth, the bundle can be
divided and the cuttings potted up individually.

⬈ Stem cuttings which are thick and fleshy like this
C. rupicola, require at least four weeks to callous.

⬇ *Ceropegia woodii* (chain of hearts) likes to be kept
moist during propagation. Stem cuttings need no
callous time. Small tubers can be dug and replanted
separately; but for best results they should have a
stem with some leaves attached.

Conophytum

A large genus of at least fifty species, all of which come from the winter rainfall areas of South Africa and Namibia. Conophytums are miniature mesembs which have a definite dormant season during late spring and early summer.

Conophytums can be easily propagated from individual 'head' cuttings. Each head is composed of two fused leaves which contain within them the tissue which will produce the new leaves for the following season. Cut the thin lower stem as close as possible to the individual head to expose the youngest stem tissue as this is the quickest way to produce new roots. Larger clumps can also be cut but these will be slower to form roots. The best time for cuttings is in late summer when the plants are just breaking into flower and growth. Remove any flowers early as these will dry out the body of the cutting. Fresh cuttings should be calloused for about a week and then lightly pushed into damp potting mix to develop roots. Cuttings should be kept in a cool, slightly humid and shaded location.

Conophytums grow easily but very slowly from seeds. Treat the seeds as described on page 59, but plant them in early spring or autumn instead of during the warmer months. Conophytums do not appreciate high temperatures when in growth.

⯅ During summer, conophytums stop growing and are covered with a dry skin which protects them from drying out and from the summer sun.

⯆ A conophytum in its winter growth stage.

⯆ Take short cuttings. Single heads will root quicker than multiple heads.
Insert: Very sharp scissors are best for the job.

Cotyledon

A small genus of about ten species. Except for one subtropical species, cotyledons prefer less humid environments. They are mostly propagated from stem cuttings taken during the warmer months. New roots develop very slowly, often taking one or two months.

Most cotyledons, especially those with succulent stems, can be propagated from stem cuttings with only two leaves attached. Lower stem cuttings are possible, even without leaves. Sections of the lower stem can be laid lengthwise on potting mix or slightly pressed in. Do not allow these cuttings to dry out completely.

Many cotyledon leaves will grow roots but these seldom, if ever, produce plantlets even though they can grow for many months as single leaves with a healthy root system. Leaves with a short section of stem attached will grow, but this is actually a form of stem cutting (see photo).

Cotyledon seeds are dust-like and should be treated as described on page 59. Cross-pollination from different clones is necessary for seeds to be produced.

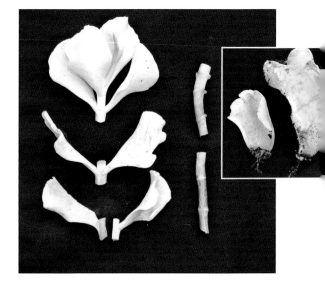

⬆ *Cotyledon orbiculata.* A few options for long and leggy stem cuttings. The upper stem cutting will establish first. The woody stem on the right will be slow, but will produce a few offsets. A section of stem has been split with a leaf attached to each piece. These will root and grow into a new plant. Insert: Single leaves can grow roots but unlike echeverieas, will not develop plantlets.

⬇ This *Cotyledon macrantha* has had its leafy upper portion removed and replanted as a stem cutting. The remaining stem is now producing numerous offsets.

Crassula

A very large and diverse genus of about 200 succulent species ranging in size from tall shrubs to miniature species barely larger than a thumbnail.

Those species which branch and are shrub-like are easily propagated from stem cuttings taken during the warmer months. Most species produce roots quickly. The smaller, slower growing species should have the tip cut off and transplanted as a stem cutting. This forces the main plant to produce side stems which it would otherwise not readily do.

Compact and smaller crassulas often have leaves which overlap each other tightly. Water is easily trapped between the leaves, creating an ideal location for infectious fungi which cause rot. Stem cuttings of these types require the lowest leaves to be peeled away and discarded (see photo) before planting so that only the stem is in contact with damp potting mix.

Many crassula species will grow from leaf cuttings. The larger and thicker the leaf, the easier they will be to root and care for. The miniature species can be difficult to propagate from leaf cuttings, mainly because they often dry out well before enough roots are produced for water replacement. If kept in too humid an environment, they will often become fungus infected and rot.

In the great majority of species, cross-pollination is necessary for seed production. The seeds are dust-like in size. For more information on how to raise small seeds, see page 59.

⭹ Crassula stem cuttings are especially vulnerable to bending if left horizontal while callousing. Rotate them daily or keep them upright in dry potting mix while callousing.

⭹ Fresh crassula stem cuttings having their lower leaves peeled away before callousing. This will help prevent stem rot when stems are pushed into damp potting mix.

Cucurbits
(such as *Gerrardanthus, Ibervillea, Kedrostis, and Momordica*)

▲ Male (lower) and female flowers from *Momordica rostrata*. Note the newly fertilised female flower (arrow).
Insert: Fruit from a kedrostis. Most cucurbit fruits turn orange or red when ripe.

There are at least twenty genera of cucurbits that produce a caudex which are of interest to succulent collectors. Most of these are obscure and seldom offered for sale to collectors other than as habitat collected specimens but they may be available as seedlings through mail order sources.

Some genera, such as *Gerrardanthus*, will grow from stem cuttings. Stem sections (150-200 mm long) should only be cut during the warmer months. Most of the leaves should be immediately removed. If kept shaded and in a humid atmosphere, they may produce roots in about two weeks. It will take at least three or four years before such cuttings develop an attractive caudex.

Cucurbits can be easily grown from seeds, most of which are the size of cucumber seeds. Some are round, others flattened and narrow. Most genera have male and female flowers on separate plants and will need to be cross-pollinated. Seeds should be sown as described on page 57. Seedlings grow quickly and often produce a vine over 1 metre long within their first growing season.

▼ These fast growing cucurbit seedlings are only six weeks of age and already have a stout succulent stem developing.

Dudleya

A genus of about fifty species, most of which are native to the winter rainfall areas of California. Dudleyas are rosette forming and most will branch with age. Stem cuttings are best taken from midautumn to early winter. These will grow roots but some will be very slow, especially if the cutting tissue is more than a few years old. Take short cuttings, as older stem tissue roots poorly. Do not try to propagate dudleyas during summer.

Even though dudleyas are closely related to echeverias, they will not grow from leaf cuttings.

Seed is the easiest way to propagate the single rosette types, such as the popular *D. brittonii*. Seeds ripen in midsummer. Examine a single fruit before picking to make certain the inner portion is as dry as the outside appears (see photo, page 101). Plant the seeds in early to midautumn and keep the seedlings moist throughout winter and spring. By early summer, the seedlings should have eight to ten leaves and will begin to go dormant (thus requiring no water) over summer. It is normal for most of the seedling leaves to wither away over summer.

⤒ *Dudleya farinosa* seedlings only grow quickly during cooler weather. Grow them damp and in a free draining potting mix.

▸▸ Two *Dudleya* species. The one in the foreground has had its growing upper portion removed as a cutting. The remaining stem is resprouting with lots of new shoots. When large enough to handle, these can be cut away and treated as stem cuttings. Any cuttings taken should be planted immediately in damp potting mix, without any callous time.

Echeveria

A large diverse genus of at least 130 species, many of which are obscure and seldom available. Most of the hundreds of named echeverias and cultivars in cultivation are hybrids created from only a handful of colourful species.

The erect, shrubby echeverias are mainly propagated from stem cuttings. The freely off-setting types are normally propagated from offsets which can develop roots while still on the parent plant. The single headed types may occasionally produce one or two offsets. Plants can be forced to produce numerous offsets or side stems through apical coring (page 42) or head cutting (page 24).

Most of the smaller growing types will propagate easily from leaves (see page 30). The 'fancy' hybrids, many of which have curly, bumpy or cabbage-like leaves, are difficult to grow from leaf cuttings. During flowering, the large fleshy leaflets from the flower stalk can be carefully peeled away and treated as leaf cuttings (see page 36). This method is only moderately successful. Alternatively, remove the flowers from a flower stalk while still in bud and continue to do so throughout the flowering season. The flower stalk may respond by producing plantlets from the axis where the buds originally formed. A third method involves removing all flowers and buds, then cutting the mature leafy flower stalk into several segments and treating these stalks as cuttings. Thick stems with plump leaflets work best. Clean tools are needed to avoid virus contamination, especially when taking echeveria cuttings.

Many echeverias can also be propagated from seeds. See page 59 for information on sowing small seeds.

✥ Echeverias flower very regularly when grown outdoors. Hybrid seeds will develop when birds and insects cross-pollinate the different species.

✥ Small cuttings grow roots faster than larger ones.

✥ *Echeveria 'Blue Curls'* grown in shade with high nitrogen fertiliser. This forces the stems to stretch, leading to easy and regular stem cuttings.

Epiphyllum, Schlumbergera (Zygocactus), Rhipsalis and Hylocereus

These tropical cactus are mostly epiphytes, naturally living high in the branches in thick, shady forests. All propagate very easily from stem cuttings taken in late spring and, to a lesser degree, early autumn. For all smaller species with multiple segments (for example schlumbergera), it is best to take fresh green cuttings at the segment joints. Try to take two to four segments per cutting. It is also a good idea to plant several cuttings tightly as a clump. This allows for thick growth which later appears as one bushy plant. This is how commercial nurseries propagate and grow them so well.

Epiphytic cactus with large single stem segments require a stem cutting of about 100-150 mm in length. If these cuttings are thick and fleshy, the lowest 20-30 mm of the stem cutting can be trimmed to a point to minimise rot when planted in damp potting mix. Allow cuttings to callous for one or two weeks, after which they can be planted in a potting mix that has extra compost mixed in. For stability, plant cuttings 100-200 mm deep. Prop up with stakes if necessary. Once planted, epiphytic cactus prefer to be kept in a warm humid environment, with indirect or morning sunlight only. Cuttings from epiphytic cactus root and grow very quickly in warm weather and benefit from extra water and fertiliser.

Epiphyllum and hylocereus have quite large edible fruit and are occasionally raised from seeds (see page 59 for more information).

⏶ Fresh green cuttings of a schlumbergera are left to dry for 5-10 days before being planted in groups of three or more for a bushier pot.

⏷ Epiphyllums grow best from short stem cuttings (100-200 mm long).
Insert: Trim any stem cuttings that are too wide at the base.

Euphorbia

There are hundreds of succulent euphorbias which come in a huge range of sizes and forms.

Branching euphorbias will grow well from stem cuttings taken during the warmer months. Thick stemmed cuttings will need a callous time of 1-3 weeks.

The leafy, thin stemmed species such as *E. milii* (crown of thorns) grow quickly from cuttings but require a humid atmosphere to keep them from drying out until the roots form.

When cut, euphorbias bleed a milky white sap which is toxic in most species. A few species will cause permanent blindness if sap gets into the eyes. .Always wear gloves when propagating and never wipe near your eyes or mucus membranes as this can cause extreme pain for hours. Any areas of contact with skin or eyes should be immediately flushed with cold water. Some people are also sensitive to the vapour from euphorbia sap and may suffer throat or lung irritation. Always take cuttings in a well ventilated area where vapour cannot accumulate. Use extreme caution when cutting euphorbias!

Euphorbias generally grow well from seeds. Female plants set fruit only after receiving pollen from a male flower. Those species which have complete flowers (containing both male and female parts) can set seeds readily with the help of pollinating insects. Many euphorbia seeds germinate better when stored for a year. See page 57 for more information on seed raising.

⬆ Euphorbia seeds often germinate irregularly. Here, several species were sown together.

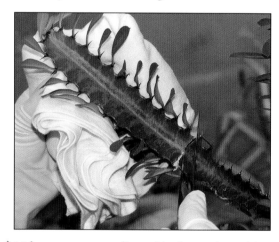

⬆ Make sure you wear disposable gloves when taking euphorbia cuttings. Keep eyes at a safe distance!

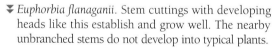

⬇ *Euphorbia flanaganii.* Stem cuttings with developing heads like this establish and grow well. The nearby unbranched stems do not develop into typical plants.

Gasteria

A genus of about thirty species. Most species grow best when given some shade.

Gasterias offset to varying degrees. The most commonly seen species are usually those that offset freely, while the rarer, and often more interesting, species seldom do. Detached offsets grow roots quickly. Species with tightly held offsets will often need to be dug up and the offsets snapped or levered off while the parent plant is held on its side or turned upside down.

Gasterias can also be propagated from leaf cuttings taken in spring. Detached leaves are best stored in a warm, dry and shaded location until plantlets are visible at the leaf base, at which time they can be placed into damp potting mix and grown on. When larger, the plantlets will need to be carefully broken off from the leaf and potted up as individual plants. With some species, leaves do not need to be complete to grow plantlets, as a section of a leaf can be grown as a cutting. This method is uncommon and is not possible with most succulents.

Sometimes small plantlets are produced as bulbils on developing flower stalks. These can be removed when the flower stalk fades and planted up and treated as a calloused cutting. Roots form quickly.

Cross-pollination is necessary for seeds to be produced. Many nectar feeding birds love gasteria flowers and inadvertently pollinate them. The fruits of gasterias turn brown when ripe and shed their seeds, which grow easily (see page 57).

⬆ Four seed grown gasteria hybrids photographed at a succulent nursery. These are going to be named as new cultivars and propagated via leaves, offsets and in the case of the lower right plant, bulbils.

⬇ *Gasteria excelsa* leaf with plantlets. The largest plantlets with roots can be removed and the leaf replanted to allow the smaller ones to develop further. Often, more plantlets will form.

Graptopetalum

A small genus of sixteen species, most of which branch freely and develop elongated stems with age. These types can be easily propagated from stem cuttings. A few species are virtually stemless but can still produce short side stems over time.

Most graptopetalums grow well from leaf cuttings taken during the warmer months. These root very quickly. At times, some graptopetalums naturally detach their leaves with only the slightest disturbance. These leaves can often be found growing for many months right where they fell, even without soil or water.

All graptopetalums need to be cross-pollinated to produce seeds. In many cases, all the plants of a given species that are commonly available will be genetically identical, having originated in the past from a single parent. Cross-pollinating such plants will not produce viable seeds. Graptopetalums have been used to produce many hybrids by cross-pollination with echeverias, leading to the hybrid genus *Graptoveria*. These cultivars generally have shorter stems than grapto-petalums. For information on seed raising, see page 59.

⯅ *Graptopetalum filiferum* is one of the species which has a very short and compact rosette, making stem cuttings difficult. Propagation by division is the easiest method. Leaves will root and form plantlets but keep these in a shaded and somewhat humid atmosphere as their small size makes them prone to drying out before they can grow functioning roots.

⯆ Graptopetalums and their hybrids can often be confused with echeverias. One of the most obvious differences is in the flowers. Graptopetalums have an open flower with petals radiating out. Echeveria flowers (insert) usually hang bell-like, with their petals only partly open.

Haworthia

A large genus of at least forty species and hundreds of subspecies and forms. All prefer light shade.

Most haworthias produce numerous offsets which can be removed when half the size of the adult. Some species produce so many offsets that they form clumps which can be easily divided. The less offsetting species are some of the most desirable and attractive types. Some produce only one offset every few years. Offsets that are tightly held on the parent plant need to be levered off. This may require some force. In such cases, the plant is best removed from the pot and dealt with from the side.

A few haworthias, such as *H. tesselata*, grow from rhizomes which should be removed when at least one-third the size of the parent plant.

Haworthias can be propagated by leaf cuttings. In most cases, complete leaves are necessary for plantlets to form. Obtaining complete leaves can be difficult as they often break while being peeled away from the stem. A scalpel can be used to sever the clasping leaf base on one side as this makes it easier to peel away. Old leaves which are beginning to yellow or are shrunken will not grow new plants, so discard these and work your way up the stem to the plumper, younger leaves. Leaves can take months to grow roots, so be patient.

Mature flower stalks occasionally produce one or two plantlets. Remove these once the flower stalks dries and treat as stem cuttings. For information on seed raising, see page 59.

⬆ *Haworthia tesselata* is one of the few haworthias which produces rhizomes. The offsets shown here are all produced from rhizomes, some of which can come up 300 mm from the parent plant.

⬇ An attractive *Haworthia truncata* hybrid which rarely produces offsets. The offset in the foreground is the first in three years and is an ideal size for removal.

Kalanchoe

A large genus of at least eighty species of leaf succulents. Most are from tropical or semi-tropical habitats and prefer humid, warm to hot summers with mild winters.

Most species of *Kalanchoe* propagate easily from stem cuttings which should be taken during the warmer months. The thicker stemmed species should be calloused for at least a week prior to being placed into damp potting mix. Some of the thin-stemmed species root readily and can be potted up immediately after being cut.

Many kalanchoes can be propagated from leaf cuttings. Some of the larger leafed species, such as the popular *K. beharensis*, will grow plantlets from along the veins of a cut leaf. Cutting a leaf into smaller sections or scoring it (see photo page 32) will result in multiple propagations from a single leaf or even part of a leaf.

Some kalanchoes (all *Bryophyllum* species are now within *Kalanchoe*) such as the well known *K. daigremontiana* and *K. tubiflora*, are strong growers which produce hundreds of plantlets along their leaf edges. They should really be called 'mother of millions' instead of 'mother of thousands'. Because of their rapid reproduction, these plants have become weeds in frost-free areas. We do not recommend propagating these species in areas with mild to warm winters because of their weed potential.

Kalanchoes need to be cross-pollinated for seeds to set. Seeds are almost dust-like and should be planted at the beginning of the warmest months (see page 59).

⚓ *Kalanchoe beharensis* (oak leaf form). A basic leaf cutting has grown several new plants which can now be divided and grown independently.

⚓ Many kalanchoes (as well as cotyledons) can be grown from short sections of stem. This works best if leaves are attached. Here, a single stem node of *Kalanchoe orygalis* has been split in two, leaving one leaf attached to a stem section. Each section can produce a new plant, as shown in the centre. Insert: *Kalanchoe orygalis*.

Lithops
(including *Lapidaria* and *Dinteranthus*)

'Living stones' and their close relatives are extreme succulents which generally have only one pair of functioning leaves per stem at any one time. There are about thirty species but many varieties and colour forms.

Lithops eventually form multiheaded clumps. It is possible to take stem cuttings from these during the warmer months, but it is risky as the cuts needed to separate the individual heads can easily become infected, leading to the death of the cutting as well as the main plant.

Lithops are almost always propagated via seeds. Cross-pollination is necessary for seeds to be produced. The yellow flowering and white flowering species tend not to hybridise. If pollination is successful, a fruit will develop and be retained between the leaves. It takes about five months to ripen, at which time the fruit will open slightly. Water causes the fruit to open fully. The seeds will then easily dislodge from the fruit. Pick the fruit when it looks dry and turns brown. Dry them out completely, then break the hard fruit with a pair of pliers. The small, tan-coloured seeds can be sieved free from the crushed remains. Lithops seeds benefit from ageing for a year. Sow them as described on page 59. Seedlings prefer being kept constantly damp for the first six months of their lives, after which they will require a gradual period of drying out.

Dinteranthus seeds, once sown, benefit from extreme heat (59°C over at least a week) to trigger germination.

⊼ *Lithops olivacea* in flower. Note last year's seed pod.

⊻ (left) Quartz gravel can be used to cover the tiny seeds and tender seedlings of dinteranthus.
(right) Gravel blown away to reveal tender seedlings which grow well under the protection of the gravel.

⊻ Crowded *Lapidaria margaretae* seedlings. The reddish colour (top right) is a sign of stress from too much sun, lack of fertiliser or lack of water.

Mammillaria

This large genus of approximately 200 species is by far the most popular genus of cactus with collectors.

Mammillarias are mainly propagated from stem cuttings or raised from seeds in spring. Smaller mammillarias that produce multiple new stems each year like *M. prolifera* and *M. gracilis*, need only a gentle nudge to cause stems to break away from the main body. If stems come away easily, plant them as cuttings immediately. A day or two to dry out may be necessary in very mild or cool climates. Larger-bodied mammillarias seldom produce offsets that detach easily. New stems are difficult to detach and will require secateurs or a fine saw blade. Stem cuttings are best taken at the joint connecting the cutting to the main stem. A callousing period of two to six weeks is advisable.

Solitary, or mostly solitary stemmed mammillarias can grow to be tall, and eventually they lean over or fall. These can have the upper portion cut off and treated as a stem cutting. The lower stem usually recovers, eventually forming multiple heads. The length of the stem cutting should be two or three times the width of the stem; any longer and the stem will be woody and will not root easily. Callous time for these large cuttings will need to be at least three months. In colder climates, growers leave them for a whole season to dry out and only plant them the following spring.

The bulk of mammillarias grow well from seeds (see page 59). Only a few are considered difficult to grow. Difficult species are usually miniatures that develop thick tap roots. Such species are often grafted.

⊼ *Mammillaria prolifera* gets its name from its rapid proliferation. Flowers, fruit and seed set more readily than most other cactus. This species is also very easy to propagate from stem cuttings which fall apart without the need for any cutting tools.

⊻ *Mammillaria guelzowiana* grows thick side stems which do not come away without tearing or cutting large portions of plant flesh. Use a thumb to first lever and then roll the side stem, which usually breaks away. A sharp blade can also be used to slice the side stem off cleanly.

Miniature mesembs

(including *Aloinopsis, Faucaria, Fenestraria, Frithia, Gibbaeum, Pleiospilos* and *Titanopsis*)

There are at least thirty genera in this group which propagate in a similar manner. Many of these are obscure and seldom propagated, even though the process is quite easy.

Most miniature mesembs form small compact clumps which in time can grow up to 250 mm in diameter. Stem cuttings are possible but each must be composed of at least one growing 'head'. Faucarias and gibbaeums are the easiest to take cuttings from because they have short stems beneath their leaves. These can be seen when the plant is unpotted. Cut the stems as close to the leaves as possible as the older stem tissue is much slower to form roots. Take cuttings during the warmer months, callous for ten days and then lay the cuttings on damp potting mix. Do not bury the stems as they can rot easily if kept too damp. Taking cuttings from the other genera is more difficult because they have short stems.

Most miniature mesembs can be easily grown from seeds. Flowers need to be cross-pollinated to produce viable seeds. Some types set seeds readily outdoors. Treat the seeds as described on page 59. Seedlings germinate and grow quickly, often reaching flowering size in only one or two years.

⤒ Faucaria stem cuttings should be short and without any lower woody stem.

⤒ A close-up view of mesemb fruit in the garden. Ripe seed pods open during rainy weather and close when dry again. Some seeds spill out at each time.

⤓ *Pleiospilos simulans* with some old fruit from the previous year's flowering. These can be crushed and sieved to separate the seeds, which will still germinate well.

Notocactus

This popular genus is most noted as singular stemmed round bodied cactus that have large golden-yellow flowers. On sunny days in early to midspring, several of these flowers can cover and hide the entire cactus body. While a few have other coloured flowers, yellows are the dominant colour.

Several species of *Notocactus* are multi-stemmed, including N. *magnificus* and N. *scopa*, but these are in the minority. Stem cuttings of these taken in midspring will need three to four weeks' callous time before planting. Cuttings need to be taken as complete stems. Be careful not to just lever or pull them apart, as internal damage often occurs with notocactus using this method. Instead, use a sharp knife or saw blade and cut where the stems join the parent plant.

Notocactus are all commonly and easily raised from seeds. Seedlings grow quickly and are able to flower within two or three years. It is advisable to propagate all single stemmed notocactus from seeds every five to ten years, as plants older than this become unsightly and eventually weaken and wither.

Notocactus are self-fertile and seed set on most outdoor grown plants is very common. The fruit is not very obvious and ripens suddenly without a noticeable change. If collecting notocactus seeds, the fruit must be checked daily and picked as soon as the first sign of seed spillage occurs. Many notocactus seedlings tolerate wetter conditions and higher humidity than many other cactus and are a good beginner's plant for seed raising.

⏶ Well grown cactus seedlings show even growth and a compact form. They should be green with a tinge of red. The red colour indicates sun hardening and also ensures that the seedling develops a thick and disease resistant skin.
Insert: These seedlings are too red, indicating too much sun.

⏷ Notocactus seedlings are easy to grow. If sown densely, cactus seedlings will eventually buckle upward. These should have been pricked out and potted up or retrayed before this occurs.
Insert: Notocactus can flower in two years when raised from seeds.

Opuntia, Cylindropuntia and *Tephrocactus*

Opuntia and related genera are mostly spiny, sculptural shrubs and trees. Aside from having obvious spines, they also possess tiny detachable barbed hair spines called glochids, which make handling and propagating a real challenge. These glochids are found in little clusters at the base of larger spines or where larger spines would normally be found, and also profusely cover the fruit.

Propagation of opuntias and related genera is usually by stem cuttings of single sections cut or broken where they join each other. Stem cuttings of about 100 mm in length from thin stemmed cylindropuntias can be cut using a sharp knife. Callous time before planting varies greatly with this group, but at least ten days is advisable. Cuttings of the slower growing compact globular species (such as some tephrocactus) prefer not to be planted deeply. Rather, rest them in shallow depressions in potting mix.

Raising opuntias from seeds is not easy. Opuntia seeds are large, hard skinned and can be very slow to germinate. Some can take one to three years. Sow as for large seeds (see page 57). Most species germinate best when given a wide daily temperature variation. Some of the more difficult to grow species from alpine environments need a damp, cold winter and are best kept outside during this period.

⤒ Assorted opuntia species which were all grown from single stem cuttings (segments) taken in late spring. Single segments are often referred to as opuntia 'pads'.

⤓ A slow growing miniature tephrocactus has had single stems split into halves and then grafted on to the hardier and faster growing *Opuntia ficus-indica*. The rootstock makes the tephrocactus grow faster and produce more side stems than normal.

Pachyphytum

All of the fifteen species have very fleshy or compact leaves which are generally cylindrical in shape.

Pachyphytums develop short multiple stems from which stem cuttings can be taken and rooted down during the warmer months.

All species of *Pachyphytum* grow well from leaf cuttings which are best taken during late spring. Leaves break free of the stem easily. Most species can be planted in or placed on dry potting mix where they will root within two or three weeks or they can be left lying in a warm, shady place until they show roots.

Pachyphytum seeds are dust-like and can only be produced from unrelated clones by cross-pollination. It is not uncommon for a grower to buy two specimens from different sources only to find that both have long ago originated as cuttings from the same parent plant. Such plants cannot produce viable seeds by attempts at cross-pollination. For more seed raising information, see page 59.

✦ *Pachyphytum compactum*. Short fat leaves and stems are common to the whole genus. The leaves shown here fell off with a slight touch. Do not plant or bury them; rather, rest them on soil or potting mix as seen here, where they will start growing roots and plantlets.

✦ *Pachyphytum oviferum* grows well from stem cuttings. Insert: Moved to a warm and shady place for two weeks, this stem has stretched, exposing it for easy cutting.

Pachypodium

A small genus of about fifteen species, most of which are from the tropics or subtropics.

Pachypodiums are usually grown from seeds. The pollination of pachypodiums requires a special technique (see page 54). Most species (a clear exception is *P. geayi*) have seeds with short viability and will lose their ability to germinate within months of harvesting, particularly if stored poorly (see page 52 for comments on seed storage). Much of the seed of the more common species that is available commercially comes from plants in cultivation and this fresh or well stored seed has a better germination rate than poorly stored and often older seed that has been habitat collected. Seeds should be sown at the beginning of the warmest months (the exception is the cooler growing *P. namaquanum*). See page 57 for information on seed raising.

Pachypodiums can be grown from stem cuttings, which root quickly in hot, humid conditions. Plants grown from cuttings do not usually develop stout stems or the same growth form as the parent plant.

P. succulentum and *P. bispinosum* can be propagated from root cuttings (see page 38). The thicker the root, the more likely it will survive and produce new shoots.

It may be possible to propagate the thicker and larger leafed species, such as *P. geayi*, from leaf cuttings.

⯅ Three species of pachypodium seedlings that are now almost two years old. Under hot, tropical conditions pachypodiums will grow much faster.

⯆ From left to right: Seedlings of *Pachypodium horombense, P. rosulatum, P. bispinosum* and *P. namaquanum*. Note that the first two species have fibrous roots while the others have long, thick taproots. Pachypodiums which develop tap roots need to be sown and grown in deep pots to allow for the best development.

Rebutia, Sulcorebutia and Aylostera

All three genera are small, compact and mound forming with profuse flowering in a spectacular range of colours. With a few exceptions, they are all easy to grow in mild to cool climates and flower well when grown in pots. Each year, new side stems will develop until a dense mound of stems up to 300 mm or more in diameter is reached.

Rebutias and related genera propagate easily from offsets or stem cuttings taken in early spring. These need to be cut cleanly where the side stems join the parent plant. Try to carefully lever off side stems as these sometimes break away easily. A callous time of two to four weeks is advisable.

Sulcorebutias are a finer, smaller and more decorative group than the other two genera. A longer callous time of three to six weeks is advisable. All rebutias and related genera grow well from seeds planted in mid-spring.

Both rebutias and aylosteras can flower within two years from seed with sulcorebutias usually taking a year longer. It is common for plants of only 30 mm in diameter to flower. The ripe fruit is small and usually hidden around the base of the plant. Detach fruit before it splits and allow them to dry out further indoors. See page 59 for seed germination information.

⮝ *Sulcorebutia rauschii*. Once stem cuttings establish a good root system, they usually swell with a growth surge for a year or two, growing faster than the parent plant (insert).

⮟ *Aylostera pulvinata* is fast growing from offsets taken in spring. Single stems pull apart easily and can be planted after a week of callous time. After one year offsets are often large enough to flower and offset profusely on their own.

Sansevieria

A genus of about forty species, many of which have long, strappy or cylindrical leaves. Sansevierias are mostly grown for their leaf markings and there are many variegated forms available.

Some species form dense clumps requiring occasional division. Other sansevierias have more open clumps where each growing head is attached by an underground rhizome. Such clumps are best cut or divided during the warmer months. If grown in tropical areas, sansevierias can be propagated throughout the year.

Most sansevierias grow from leaf cuttings (see right). The variegated forms usually do not retain their leaf colours when grown from leaf cuttings; instead, they revert to their normal green form.

Seeds are not usually produced under garden or home conditions. If flowering does occur, cross-pollination is necessary to produce seeds. The fruit usually contain a single seed which is about the size of a small pea. Seeds may require some sanding or chipping with a knife to remove a portion of the hard seed coat before planting.

◥ Sansevieria leaves can be cut into segments. If the conditions are right, each segment will produce multiple plantlets.

◥ Sansevieria leaves showing a well developed root system and the beginnings of plantlets. Note how the leaves have now become dark green from the nutrients absorbed through the roots.

▶▶ Twelve months after cutting. One of the leaf sections has developed three plantlets. The largest of these can be severed from the parent leaf and potted up. The parent leaf can be replanted as it may produce additional plantlets.

Sedum

A very diverse and large genus of several hundred species and subspecies. Sedums come in a huge variety of shapes, sizes and growth forms so it is difficult to generalise about the genus.

All of the branching sedums can be propagated from stem cuttings, which are best taken in spring. Those species which lose all their leaves and die right back to the ground annually can be divided at the roots in winter or early spring.

Sedums with large and thick leaves will propagate well from leaf cuttings, which are best taken from spring to autumn.

Miniature ground cover sedums can be propagated by lifting a clump out of the ground by the roots and literally shaking the plant until pieces of stem and leaves break off. This can be done over a bare patch of garden that needs carpeting with sedums. Immediately sprinkle some topsoil over the area covered with sedum pieces (but do not bury them) and keep the area moist. Within two or three months there should be a carpet of sedums.

Seeds of sedums are dust-like and require cross-pollination to produce fertile fruit. The fruit is small and will split open when fully dry, quickly spilling their seeds, so harvest promptly. Sow the small seeds as described on page 59.

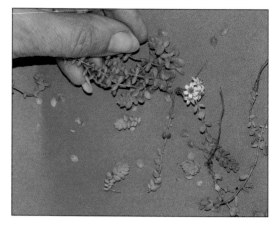

⬆ Many smaller thick leafed sedums will propagate well by just shaking or breaking pieces off. This demonstration was done over paper, but is usually done directly over a garden bed. Pieces usually grow where they fall.

⬇ *Sedum 'Autumn Joy'* dies down to ground level during its winter dormancy. The underground clumps can be divided at this time. In spring, it can also be grown from stem cuttings.
Insert: Flowers.

Sempervivum

A large genus of about sixty species. All species propagate well from offsets which develop from the almost stemless rosettes. Most offsets are produced on short runners which slowly disintegrate as the offsets develop their own roots. Offsets are best removed in spring or autumn. The larger hybrids tend not to develop many offsets and it may be necessary to core the plant (see page 42) in order to force it to offset profusely.

Sempervivums do not grow readily from leaves, but they can be encouraged to do so if a small portion of stem remains attached to the leaf. This can usually only be accomplished by completely cutting up a rosette in spring. Use a scalpel to cut the stem in to very small sections with leaves attached.

Sempervivum seeds are seldom commercially available. If you have the patience and space to grow hundreds of seedlings then seed raising of hybrids may produce a new, superior and potentially valuable hybrid. Start with attractive parent plants which are then cross-pollinated. Raise as many hybrid seedlings as you can for one year, evaluate them and only keep a few of the very best seedlings to propagate from. The rest will probably be much less attractive than either parent so do not use these for propagation. Sow seeds as described on page 59.

⬆ Sempervivums are often referred to as 'hen and chickens' as they grow profuse offsets that cluster around parent plants.

⬇ For sempervivums which offset poorly, cut away any immature offsets early as this will cause the remaining stems to offset profusely.

Senecio

This very large genus has seventy succulent species. Some of these are sometimes classified as *Notonia* or *Kleinia*. The succulent members of the genus are very diverse in leaf shapes and growth habit.

The shrubby, freely branching species can be easily propagated from stem cuttings. Clumps can be divided. The most common species (*S. mandraliscae* and *S. serpens*) prefer to be propagated in the cooler months. The creeping species, such as *S. pendula*, are propagated from stem cuttings taken during the warmer months. If stems tend not to branch naturally, try pinching the tips out to force the stems to branch. The caudiciform species grow easily from stem cuttings taken in the warmer months and will produce a caudex after a few years.

Senecio serpens produces short rhizomes and these can be cut once the new plants emerge above ground. *S. serpens* will also grow from stem cuttings which can be planted immediately as they normally do not require callousing.

Senecios do not propagate easily from leaf cuttings, even though some will grow a few roots.

Senecios flower regularly in cultivation. Each flower produces a dandelion-like cluster of dried flower remains which are blown apart by the wind. Unless cross-pollinated, there will not be any seeds. This is because most of the plants in cultivation are genetically identical, having been propagated from cuttings. If seed is obtained, see page 57 for information on seed raising.

⯭ Assorted senecio flower buds, flowers and, on the right, a mature seeding head ready for dispersal. Even though they flower readily, seed set is rare on cultivated plants.

⯯ *Senecio mandraliscae* grows well from stem cuttings taken during cooler months. Cuttings from new growth are quick to form roots. Older lower stem cuttings may be a little slow to establish but are still worthwhile. Leaves alone are not recommended.

Stapelia
and related genera

Stapelia, *Huernia* and *Caralluma* are the largest genera in this group of leafless stem succulents. There are hundreds of species, many of which have showy flowers.

Stapeliads propagate easily from stem cuttings, which should be taken during the warmer months. Some species can be divided without resorting to cutting. Many others have stems which need to be cleanly cut. If stems are cut, they need to be calloused for a week or two. Stem cuttings which detach easily or which have roots can be planted immediately by only burying the roots. Any stems without roots will quickly grow new roots on their lower surfaces. The stems should not be planted with the ends buried in to potting mix. Instead, simply lay the stems on the surface of the potting mix. For longer stems, prop up with a small stake or use wooden skewers as supports until established. Only the roots should be placed in to the potting mix as damp stems rot easily.

Stapeliads require cross-pollination for seed set. Pollination is a specialised procedure and cannot be carried out with a small brush. Sometimes flies initiate pollination, in which case fruit develop as 'seed horns'. When ripe, these split open. The seeds are attached to fluffy hairs which are dispersed by the wind. Cover the fruit with netting or gauze material to catch the ripe seeds.

⬆ A selection of stapeliads showing the variety of forms possible. The joint stemmed types shown at the top are the easiest to propagate. Cuttings should have two or more stem segments for best results.
Insert: Stapelia stems grow horizontally out from an existing stem. Roots form naturally on the underside of each segment.

⬇ Stapeliads all produce fruit which normally have two 'horns'. These split open when ripe, releasing the seeds for the wind to distribute. Net fruit before this happens!
Insert: Seeds at near actual size.

Trichocereus
and related genera

This genus of approximately forty species has recently been expanded to include *Helianthocereus* and other genera. *Trichocereus* are mostly columnar in growth habit, ranging up to 10 metres in height.

Some shorter *Trichocereus* species produce numerous new stems, which can be detached with a little levering where they join the main plant body. Within a week these stem cuttings can be planted separately. A few *Trichocereus* species grow as clumps which can be divided at the base. This may require large clumps to be lifted out to expose their roots and then slowly levering sections apart. Ideally some attached roots will come away with each stem or section. Stem cuttings or divisions can be left out of the ground with roots exposed for one to two weeks before replanting. Taller or narrower stemmed trichocereus are best propagated from stem cuttings (100-200 mm lengths) taken with a large knife or fine saw from the uppermost or freshest areas in late spring. Allow to callous for 4-6 weeks.

All trichocereus grow well from seeds; however, many seedlings are very slow for the first year, after which they grow more rapidly. Some trichocereus are self-fertile. Seed from garden plants is common but much of this is likely to be hybrid seed. See page 59 for seed germination information.

⤒ Trichocereus seedlings are among the fastest growing of cactus. Here, they are several times larger than the other cactus seedlings, some of which are infected with a soil borne fungus. The healthy seedlings should be immediately removed and repotted individually if large enough. Destroy infected plants.

⤓ The larger of these eighteen month old trichocereus seedlings are ready to be potted up. The smaller ones will be group potted where they will grow for another season before being potted up individually. Note the small seedling at the base of one of the larger plants. This latecomer is the result of uneven germination, perhaps due to the seeds being old.

Tylecodon

All forty or so species in this genus are winter gowers, mostly with deciduous leaves and swollen trunks. Tylecodons are closely related to *Cotyledon* (hence the anagram), the only difference being that they are deciduous and develop swollen stems.

Most tylecodons can be propagated from stem cuttings, which should be taken in early autumn and allowed to callous for a few weeks. The larger the cut surface, the longer the callous time. Avoid taking cuttings from stems that have flowers or fruit developing. Alternatively, cut these away before taking cuttings.

Tylecodons usually flower during early summer and the fruit is dry by midautumn. Cross-pollination is required, but insects may pollinate the flowers naturally, especially if plants are kept outdoors during their flowering time. Sow the small seeds as described on page 59 but do so during early autumn instead of spring or early summer. Keep seedlings damp throughout winter and spring, gradually easing off watering as summer approaches. Seedlings, as well as adult plants, shed all their leaves during summer, when they should be kept dry. Tylecodons can go without a drop of water all summer while they are dormant. While they can tolerate misting or an occasional watering during summer, regular watering during this time will only harm them.

Tylecodons do not grow from leaves.

⬙ Fruit of *Tylecodon* (and *Dudleya*) take a long time to ripen. Here, the dry looking fruit are shown to be still unripe on the inside. Check fruit to make sure they are fully ripe before picking.

⬙ A selection of tylecodon species, showing the diversity of growth forms. In general, the thinner the stem, the easier they will be to propagate from stem cuttings.

How to propagate eighty popular succulents

plant	how it spreads	methods of propagation*	when to propagate
Aeonium arboreum	stems	stem cuttings	not summer
Aeonium tabuliforme	solitary	mostly leaves, few offsets	not summer
Aeonium 'Tricolor'	stems	stem cuttings	not summer
Aeonium 'Zwartkop'	stems	stem cuttings	not summer
Agave americana	offsets, rhizomes	offsets	not winter
Agave attenuata	offsets	offsets, bulbils	spring
Agave filifera	offsets	offsets, seeds	spring, summer
Agave stricta	offsets	seeds, division	spring, summer
Agave victoriae-reginae	solitary	seeds, rarely offsets	spring, summer
Aloe ferox	solitary	seeds	spring, summer
Aloe juvenna	stems	stem cuttings	spring, summer
Aloe plicatilis	stems	seeds, stem cuttings	spring, summer
Aloe polyphylla	solitary	seeds, head cuts	spring
Aloe vera	offsets	offsets	spring, summer
Aloe x spinossissima	offsets	offsets	not winter
Aptenia cordifolia	sprawling	stem cuttings	spring, summer
Beaucarnea (Nolina) recurvata	solitary	seeds	spring
Beschorneria yuccoides	clumping	seeds, division	spring, summer
Brachychiton rupestris	solitary	seeds	spring
Carpobrotus edulis	sprawling	stem cuttings	spring, summer
Cotyledon orbiculata	sprawling	stem cuttings, seeds	spring, summer
Cotyledon macrantha	sprawling	stem cuttings	spring, summer
Crassula arborescens	stems	stem cuttings	spring, summer
Crassula falcata	stems	stem cuttings	spring, summer
Crassula ovata	stems	stem cuttings	spring, summer
Dasylirion wheeleri	mostly solitary	seeds	spring
Dioscorea elephantipes	solitary	seeds	not summer
Dorotheanthus bellidoniformis	sprawling	seeds	autumn
Doryanthes species	mostly solitary	seeds	spring
Dracaena draco	stems	seeds, stem cuttings	spring, summer
Dudleya brittonii	solitary	seeds	autumn, winter
Echeveria agavoides	few offsets	offsets, leaves	spring, summer
Echeveria 'Black Prince'	few offsets	leaves, offsets	spring, summer
Echeveria 'Blue Curl's	mostly solitary	offsets, head cuts	spring, summer
Echeveria elegans	offsets	offsets, seeds	not winter
Echeveria glauca var. *pumila*	offsets	offsets	year round
Echeveria globulosa	offsets	offsets	spring
Echeveria 'Mauna Loa'	solitary	head cuts, leaves	spring, summer
Echeveria 'Violet Queen'	offsets	offsets	not winter

* Easiest method is listed first

In most cases, related species will propagate identically to the listed species.

additional information

Fresh cuttings do not need to callous before planting.

Best in late autumn.

Fresh cuttings do not need to callous before planting.

Fresh cuttings do not need to callous before planting.

Rhizomes develop offsets, cut away when larger than 100 mm.

Bulbils on old flower stalks come away easily, as do offsets.

Blue clone does not have offsets, so raise from seeds.

Clones without offsets best, raise these from seeds.

Clones without offsets best, raise these from seeds.

Very easy and fast growing from seeds.

Callous the cuttings for 6-10 weeks before planting.

Do not propagate from diseased or virus infected plants. Seeds germinates best at 15°C.

Deheading this rare plant is a hard thing to do but worth the effort.

Prefers warmer weather, protect from frost.

Takes light frost, produces lots of offsets.

Sprawling stems can be buried as they grow. As roots form, take cuttings.

Bury the seeds slightly and keep wet for three weeks.

Easy and fast growing from seeds.

Plants develop long taproots, use deep pots or containers. Seedlings are fast growers.

Sprawling stems can root naturally along the ground.

Young stems work best, avoid old wood. Some clones grow easily from seeds.

Young green stems work best, avoid old wood.

Larger stems and trunk cuttings can also be used as cuttings which propagate well.

Do not allow fresh cuttings to flower for the first year. Cut buds off as they appear.

Lower stems and trunk cuttings can also be used as cuttings which propagate well.

Fast and easily grown from seeds.

Shade from summer sun and heat.

Sprinkle seeds onto sunny open areas of the garden during autumn and winter for spring flowers.

Prefers well drained, deep and sandy soil.

Each fruit has only one large seeds. Cuttings are slow to establish.

Shade from summer sun and heat.

Leaves break easily. Use only plump healthy leaves which are not broken at the base.

Leaves break easily. Use only plump healthy leaves which are not broken at the base.

Few offsets. Head cuts force best offsets. Propagates very poorly from leaves.

Very easy from offsets taken in spring.

Very easy from offsets taken in spring.

Very easy from offsets taken in spring.

Head cuts force a few offsets, leaves work poorly.

Very easy from offsets taken in spring.

plant	how it spreads	methods of propagation*	when to propagate
Echeveria shaviana	mostly solitary	leaves, offsets	spring
Euphorbia caput-medusae	mostly solitary	seeds, stem cuttings	not winter
Euphorbia flanaganii	few offsets	offsets, stem cuts	not winter
Euphorbia milii	stems	stem cuttings, seeds	summer
Fockea edulis	solitary	seeds	spring, summer
Gasteria species	clumping	division, offsets	not winter
Graptoveria 'Huths Pink'	offsets	offsets, leaves	not winter
Graptopetalum paraguayense	stems	stem cuttings, leaves	not winter
Graptoveria 'Debbi'	offsets	offsets, leaves	spring, summer
Haworthia attenuata	clumping	offsets, leaves, seeds	spring to autumn
Haworthia cymbiformis	clumping	offsets, seeds	spring to autumn
Haworthia tesselata	offsets	offsets, leaves, rhizomes	not winter
Kalanchoe beharensis	mostly solitary	leaves, head cuts	spring, summer
Kalanchoe blossfeldiana	stems	stem cuttings	spring, summer
Kalanchoe tomentosa	stems	stem cuttings	spring, summer
Lampranthus species	clumping	stem cuttings	year round
Lithops species	clumps	seeds	spring
Manfreda species	clumping	divison, seeds	winter, spring
Oscularia deltoides	solitary	stem cuttings	not winter
Pachyphytum compactum	stems	leaves, stem cuttings	not winter
Pachyphytum oviferum	stems	leaves, stem cuttings	spring, summer
Pachypodium lamerei	solitary	seeds	summer
Pleiospilos species	clumps	seeds	spring, summer
Portulaca grandiflora	sprawling	seeds	spring
Portulacaria afra	sprawling	stem cuttings	not winter
Sedum dasyphyllum	sprawling	leaves, division	winter, spring
Sedum mexicanum	sprawling	leaves, stem cuttings	autumn, winter
Sedum nussbaumerianum	sprawling	stem cuttings, leaves	spring, summer
Sedum pachyphyllum	sprawling	leaves, stem cuttings	spring, autumn
Sedum rubrotinctum	sprawling	leaves, stem cuttings	spring, autumn
Sedum sieboldii	clumping	division, stem cuttings	winter, spring
Sedum spectabile	clumping	division, stem cuttings	winter, spring
Sempervivum arachnoideum	offsets	offsets	spring
Sempervivum hybrids	offsets	offsets	spring
Sempervivum tectorum	offsets	offsets, seeds	spring
Senecio mandraliscae	sprawling	stem cuttings	autumn-spring
Senecio serpens	rhizomes	stem cuttings, division	autumn-spring
Stapelia gigantea	sprawling	stem cuttings, division	summer
Yucca elephantipes	stems	stem cuttings	spring, summer
Yucca filamentosa	clumping	division, rhizomes	spring, summer
Yucca whipplei	solitary/clumping	seeds	spring, summer

* Easiest method is listed first

additional information

Leaves break easily. Use only plump healthy leaves which are not broken at the base.

Take only cuttings with existing side shoots. Only branched cuttings will develop into typical plants.

Take only cuttings with existing side shoots. Only these will develop into typical branched plants.

Heat and humidity helps in propagation.

Seedlings are fast growers. Develops a swollen trunk after only three months.

Fresh potting mix for freshly, newly divided offsets gives the best results.

Offsets are regularly produced. Leaves come away easily from the stem.

Both offset and leaf propagation are easy. Good for beginners.

Some leaves develop plants with poor colour. Destroy these and propagate from the best plants.

Provide some shade from the hot summer sun.

Provide some shade from the hot summer sun.

Slow growing offsets develop from rhizomes. Give plants a wide pot for maximum production.

Whole or cut pieces of leaves can grow new plants.

Very easy, likes warmth and humidity. Do not propagate while flowering.

Remove any flowers or buds during propagation.

Remove any flowers or buds during propagation.

Seedlings tolerate humidity for only their first three months of growth.

Divide clumps and replant immediately.

Remove any flower development during propagation.

Lower leaves come away easily and grow where they fall.

Lower leaves come away easily and grow where they fall.

Likes humidity and heat, cuttings possible when larger.

Seedlings tolerate humidity for only their first three months fo growth.

Sowing direct into the garden works well. An area receiving afternoon sun is best.

Keep cuttings warm and humid for fast root development.

Leaves break away easily and grow best where they fall. Alternatively, sprinkle onto potting mix.

Easy. Sprinkle fresh cuttings or leaves over garden bed and water.

Easy. Plant stem cuttings after several days. Leaves will grow where they fall.

Leaves break away easily and grow best where they fall. Alternatively, sprinkle onto potting mix.

Leaves break away easily and grow best where they fall. Alternatively, sprinkle onto potting mix.

Division best when plants are dormant. Stem cuttings can be taken in spring.

Division best when plants are dormant. Stem cuttings can be taken in spring.

Prolific and easy. Likes lots of fresh air, humidity causes rot.

Hybrids propagate similar to below.

Cool weather is preferred to hot or humid conditions above 25°C.

Leaves will grow roots and develop no further. Stem cuttings develop well.

Leaves will grow roots and develop no further. Stem cuttings develop well.

Lay stems on their sides rather than plant into potting mix, as buried stems rot easily.

Stem, branches or main trunk cuts from older trees will root easily.

Below ground rhizomes break apart easily.

Fast and easy growing from seeds, 5-7 years to maturity.

Propagating less common genera of succulents

Adansonia	Seeds, as per page 56. Minimum temp. 25°C. Seeds should be soaked overnight.
Aichryson	Small seeds, as per page 59. Sow in autumn, winter growers. As for *Aeonium*.
Alluaudia	Cuttings. Minimum temp. 20°C. Treat as for *Euphorbia* cuttings.
Alworthia	Offsets. Propagate spring-autumn. As for *Haworthia*.
Argyroderma	Seeds. As for Conophytum. Seedlings very hard in their first year.
Astroloba	Offsets, seeds. Propagate spring-autumn. As for *Haworthia*.
Avonia	A newer name for some *Anacampseros*.
Begonia	Cuttings, small seeds. A few succulent species, treat cuttings as for *Ceropegia*.
Bombax	Seeds, as per page 57. Minimum temp. 20°C.
Bowiea	Seeds, as per page 57. The most common species is self-fertile.
Brachystelma	Seeds, as per page 57. Minimum temp. 20°C. Forms a caudex quickly.
Brighamia	Small seeds, as per page 59. Minimum temp. 20°C. Likes humidity.
Bulbine	Division, small seeds, as per page 59. As for bulbs.
Bursera	Seeds, as per page 57. Minimum temp. 20°C.
cactus	See page 29, 63. Also check for specific genera on pages 108-109.
Caralluma	Cuttings, division, seeds. Minimum temp. 20°C. As for stapeliads.
Cheiridopsis	Small seeds, as per page 59. As for *Conophytum*, but easier and faster growing.
Chorisia	Seeds, as per page 57. Seedlings are very fast growing, transplant after 3 months.
Cissus	Stem cuttings, seeds, as per page 57. Minimum temp. 20°C.
Commiphora	Seeds, as per page 57. Minimum temp. 20°C. Sand or chip as per page 57.
Cussonia	Sand or chip as per page 57. Minimum temp. 20°C.
Cyphostemma	Seeds, as per page 57. Some species are self-fertile. Sand or chip as per page 57.
Cynanchum	Cuttings, Minimum temp. 20°C. Seeds, as per page 57. As for Ceropegia.
Decaryia	Cuttings. Minimum temp. 20°C. As for *Ceropegia* cuttings.
Delosperma	As for cuttings page 18. Small seeds, as per page 59.
Didierea	Cuttings, Seeds, as per page 57. Minimum temp. 25°C. Tubercules can be tip grafted.
Dischidia	Cuttings. Minimum temp. 20°C. As for *Ceropegia*.
Dorstenia	Small seeds, as per page 59. Minimum temp. 20°C. Some are self-fertile.
Drimia	Division, offsets. As for bulbs.
Duvalia	Cuttings, division, seeds. Minimum temp. 20°C. As for stapeliads.
Echidnopsis	Cuttings, division, seeds. Minimum temp. 20°C. As for stapeliads.
Edithcolea	Cuttings, seeds. Minimum temp. 25°C. As for stapeliads.
Ficus	Small seeds, as per page 59. Minimum temp. 20°C.
Fockea	Seeds, as per page 57. Minimum temp. 20°C. Forms a caudex quickly.
Fouquieria	Seeds, as per page 57. Minimum temp. 20°C. Slow to develop adult growth form.
Furcraea	Bulbils as per page 13.
Gasterhaworthia	Offsets. Propagate spring-autumn. As for *Haworthia*.
Gastrolea	Offsets. Propagate spring-autumn. As for *Haworthia*.
Glottiphyllum	Cuttings, seeds as per page 57. As for miniature mesembs but faster growing.
Graptoveria	Offsets, cuttings, leaves. As for *Echeveria*.
Greenovia	Small seeds, as per page 59. Sow in autumn, winter growers. As for *Aeonium*.
Hesperaloe	Division, seeds, as per page 57. Fruit common on garden grown plants.

Hoodia	Cuttings, seeds. Minimum temp. 25°C. As for stapeliads.
Hoya	Cuttings. Minimum temp. 20°C. As for *Ceropegia*. Enjoys humidity.
Huernia	Cuttings, division, seeds. Minimum temp. 20°C. As for stapeliads.
Idria	Seeds as per page 57. Fast to germinate. Keep dry and shaded during mid-summer.
Ipomoea	Seeds, as per page 57. Minimum temp. 20°C.
Jatropha	Seeds, as per page 57. Minimum temp. 20°C. Also from stem cuttings.
Jovibarba	Division, seeds. As for *Sempervivum*.
Lomatophyllum	Seeds, as per page 57. Rhizomes (page 13) for a few species. Related to *Aloe*.
Mestoklema	Small seeds, as per page 59. Cuttings as per page 18.
Monadenium	Cuttings, seeds. Minimum temp. 20°C. Enjoys humidity.
Monanthes	Division. Winter growers. As for *Aeonium*.
Operculicarya	Cuttings, seeds. Minimum temp. 20°C. Seeds may have delayed germination.
Orbea	Cuttings, division, seeds. Minimum temp. 20°C. As for stapeliads.
Orostachys	Small seeds, as per page 59. Some species produce cuttings. Dislikes summer heat.
Othonna	As per cuttings, page 18. Seeds, as per page 57. All species are winter growers.
Pachyveria	Cuttings, leaves. As per *Pachyphytum* or *Echeveria*.
Pedilanthus	Cuttings. Minimum temp. 20°C. Enjoys humidity.
Peperomia	Cuttings Most species like warmth and some shade.
Piaranthus	Cuttings, division, seeds. Minimum temp. 20°C. As for stapeliads.
Plectranthus	Cuttings. Several species can become weeds in a potted collection.
Pterodiscus	Seeds, as per page 57. Minimum temp. 20°C. Each fruit contains only four seeds.
Raphionacme	Seeds, as per page 57. Minimum temp. 20°C. Seeds fast to germinate.
Rochea	Cuttings. Small seeds, as per page 59. As for *Crassula*.
Rosularia	Offsets, cuttings. As for *Sempervivum*.
Ruschia	Cuttings. Small seeds, as for page 59.
Sarcocaulon	Seeds, as per page 57. Sow in autumn, winter growers.
Sarcostemma	Cuttings, seeds as per page 57. As per *Ceropegia*.
Sedeveria	Cuttings, leaves. As per *Graptopetalum*. Most have brittle leaves and long stems.
Seyrigia	Cuttings. Minimum temp. 20°C.
Sinningia	Small seeds, as for page 59. Small seedlings enjoy humidity as for cactus seedlings.
Sinocrassula	Cuttings, as per *Crassula*.
Stapelianthus	Cuttings, division, seeds. Minimum temp. 20°C. As for stapeliads.
Synadenium	Cuttings, Minimum temp. 20°C. Enjoys humidity.
Talinum	Small seeds, as per page 59. Flowers are self-pollinating. Fast and easy to grow.
Tavaresia	Cuttings, seeds. Minimum temp. 20°C. As for stapeliads. Cuttings rot easily.
Tradescantia	Stem cuttings, take in spring or summer, Cuttings need no callousing.
Trichocaulon	Seeds. Minimum temp. 20°C. As for stapeliads.
Trichodiadema	Small seeds, as per page 59. Cuttings.
Tylecodon	Small seeds, as per page 59. Sow in autumn, winter growers.
Uncarina	Seeds, as per page 57. Minimum temp. 20°C. Cuttings may be possible.
Xerosicyos	Cuttings, minimum temp. 20°C.

Notes:

The most common method of propagation is given first.

Temperatures refer to what is best for germinating or cutting care and not to minimum winter temperatures.

How to propagate forty less common cactus

genus	methods of propagation	difficulty	comments
Ariocarpus	seeds, grafting	hard	extremely slow
Arrojadoa	cuttings, seeds	moderate	provide extra heat and humidity
Aylostera	offsets, seeds	easy	remove any flowers during propagation
Aztekium	seeds, grafting	hard	extremely slow
Blossfeldia	grafting, offsets	hard	plants mature at 10 mm
Brasilicactus	seeds	moderate	treat as for notocactus page 90
Buiningia	mostly seeds	moderate	tropical, minimum temperature of 15°C
Cintia	grafting, offsets	moderate	overwatering causes stems to split
Cochemiea	cuttings, seeds	hard	treat as for mammillaria page 88
Corryocactus	cuttings, seeds	moderate	treat as for trichocereus page 100
Cylindropuntia	cuttings, seeds	easy	handle carefull, because of glochids.
Denmoza	seeds	moderate	treat as for trichocereus page 100
Discocactus	seeds, cuttings, grafting	moderate	tropical, minimum temperature of 15°C
Dolichothele	cuttings, seeds	easy	treat as for mammillaria page 88
Echinomastus	seeds, offsets	hard	variable genus
Encephalocarpus	seeds, grafting	hard	extremely slow
Eriocactus	seeds, offsets	moderate	treat as for notocactus page 90
Escobaria	seeds, offsets	hard	cold tolerant
Eulychnia	seeds, cuttings	hard	stems of seedlings rot easily
Ferocactus	mostly seeds	moderate	provide extra heat
Frailea	mostly seeds	moderate	short lived, repropagate regularly
Geohintonia	grafting, seeds	moderate	new to cultivation
Gymnocactus	mostly seeds	moderate	prefers light shade
Harrisia	cuttings	easy	potential weed, treat as for trichocereus
Helianthocereus	division, seeds	moderate	treat as for trichocereus page 100
Islaya	grafting, seeds	hard	true desert species
Krainzia	seeds, offsets	moderate	treat as for mammillaria page 88
Lemaireocereus	cuttings, seeds	moderate	treat as for trichocereus page 100
Lophocereus	cuttings, seeds	moderate	treat as for trichocereus page 100
Lophophora	seeds, offsets, division	moderate	illegal in many countries
Neobuxbaumia	seeds, cuttings	moderate	does well in the tropics
Obregonia	grafting, seeds	hard	prefers light shade
Pereskia	cuttings	easy	vigorous leafy stems, minimum 10°C
Rhipsalidopsis	cuttings	easy	treat as for epiphytic cactus page 81
Sclerocactus	mostly seeds	hard	germination needs cold pretreatment.
Solisia	seeds	moderate	treat as for mammillaria page 88
Tephrocactus	cuttings	moderate	handle carefully because of glochids
Turbinicarpus	seeds, grafting	hard	can flower within three years
Uebelmannia	seeds, grafting	hard	provide extra heat and humidity
Weingartia	mostly seeds	moderate	treat as for notocactus page 90

Recommended reading

Agaves, Yuccas and Related Plants. Irish, M and G. (2000). Timber Press.
A good handbook for identification, care and propagation for this specific group of plants.

Cacti for the Connoisseur – A Guide for Growers and Collectors. Pilbeam, J., (1987). Timber Press.
For collectors and growers of the less common cactus. Some are very difficult to propagate, This book gives useful information which should help.

The Cactus Primer. Gibson, A. C., & Noble, P. S. (1986). Harvard University Press.
A very technical book which mainly covers the theories behind cactus survival. It has relevance to all aspects of propagation. Seeds germination is specifically covered.

Caudiciforms and Pachycaul Succulents. Rowley, G. (1987). Strawberry Press.
A good book for propagating unusual succulent plants, with a focus on seeds grown, fat stemmed types.

Crassula A Grower's Guide. Rowley, G. (2003). Cactus & Co, Italy.
Includes propagation information on this much loved genus. Some exceptional seeds raised cultivars are one of the highlights of this book.

Hartmann and Kestyer's Plant Propagation: Principles and Practices (7th Edition) Hartmann, H. T. et al. (2001). Prentice Hall, USA.
The standard text book on propagation. Includes information on chemicals used to break seeds dormancy. Also information on the more obscure types of propagation, grafting and tissue culture.

The Illustrated Encyclopaedia of Succulents. Rowley, G. (1978). Salamander Books.
An older book that will only be available through libraries or second-hand sources. General propagation is covered, including grafting.

Plants from Test Tubes. Kyte, L. and J. (1996). Timber Press.
Lists professional organisations and suppliers of equipment needed. Has a glossary and an extended bibliography.

WWW contacts

The Cactus and Succulent Plant Mall is an internet resource for cactus and succulent-related topics. It is regularly updated with information on suppliers of plants, seeds and literature. All of the books mentioned above may be available through links from this site. It also hosts web pages for more than 100 cactus and succulent organisations worldwide. Visit it at: **www.cactus-mall.com**

Information on micro-propagation

www.succulent-tissue-culture.com
An international company dealing in rare cactus and succulents, based in the Netherlands.

www.austratec.com.au
An Australian company that sells tissue culture products (including home kits) worldwide.

Index
of plant names

Index

(also see pages 110 & 111)